K100 Course Team

Original production team

Andrew Northedge (Chair)
Jan Walmsley (Deputy Chair)
Margaret Allott (Course Manager)
Tanya Hames (Course Secretary)
Joanna Bornat
Hilary Brown
Celia Davies
Roger Gomm
Sheila Peace
Martin Robb
Deborah Cooper (VQ Centre)

Jill Alger, Julie Fletcher (Editors); Janis Gilbert (Graphic Artist); Hannah Brunt, Rob Williams (Designers); Paul Smith (Librarian); Deborah Bywater (Project Control Assistant); Ann Carter (Print Buying Controller); Pam Berry (Text Processing Services); Mike Levers (Photographer); Vic Lockwood, Alison Tucker, Kathy Wilson (BBC Producers); Maggie Guillon (Cartoonist)

Regional Education and Training Managers

Lindsay Brigham
Anne Fletcher
Carole Ulanowsky

External assessor

Professor Lesley Doyal, University of Bristol

This is the K100 core course team. Many other people also contributed to making the course and their names are given in the Introduction and Study Guide.

Revision team

Andrew Northedge (Chair)
Corinne Pennifold (Course Manager)
Christine Wild (Course Team Assistant)
James Blewett
Joanna Bornat
Hilary Brown
Sue Cusworth
Celia Davies
Marion Dunlop
Pam Foley
Tom Heller
Vijay Patel
Sheila Peace
Lucy Rai
Marion Reichart
Angela Russell
Geraldine Lee-Treweek
Danielle Turney
Jan Walmsley
Jo Warner

Hannah Brunt (Designer); Deborah Bywater (Project Control); Maggie Gullion (Cartoonist); Sarah Hack (Graphic Artist); Lucy Hendy (Compositor); Julie Fletcher, Denise Lulham (Editors).

Critical readers

Fiona Harkes, Sylvia Caveney, Gillian Thompson, Katy Sainsbury, Eunice Lumsden, Lynne Fisher, Margaret Brown, Paula Faller, Kate Stilliard

External reviewers

Professor Gordon Grant, University of Sheffield; Mary McColgan, University of Ulster; Nigel Porter, University of Portsmouth

External assessor

Professor Gordon Grant, University of Sheffield

Contents

Study skills by Andrew Northedge

Introduction

Who needs to know what?

Knowledge, as they say, is power. In any situation, unless you know what is going on you cannot act intelligently. All you can do is guess, hope for the best, and wait to see what happens. Care situations are no different. Anyone involved in care, whether as a service user or as a carer, needs all the relevant knowledge they can get.

- The more people know about the care services that are available and how to get access to them, the more intelligently they can make use of them.

- The more groups of care service users know about how services are organised and planned, the better chance they have of bringing pressure to bear to shape the services to meet their needs.

- The more carers know about those they care for, the more effectively and sensitively they can provide the care.

- The more carers can share knowledge with each other, the better they can co-ordinate the services they offer, to provide speedy, consistent and coherent care and avoid duplication of effort.

- And if care-providing organisations are to ensure that they provide high quality care that is safe and embodies the right values, they need detailed knowledge about the day-to-day activities of their care staff.

But knowledge is not only powerful.

- Knowledge can be very burdensome to those who have to record it, or make sense of it, distracting them from other duties.

- Knowledge is expensive, because it is time consuming to gather and requires storage and communication systems.

- Knowledge requires good organisation because it is only powerful when it is accessible at the time and place it is needed. Mountains of disorganised information can do more harm than good.

So we cannot simply say – the more knowledge the better. We have to think hard about what knowledge is for, then plan carefully how to collect, store and share it, so that its many benefits are balanced against its considerable costs. Finally, because knowledge is powerful, it can be dangerous, so it must be handled carefully. We all want to be sure that information about us is used responsibly and does not get into the wrong hands.

All this amounts to saying that recording, storing and communicating information plays a vital part in any system of care provision, but only if it is the right information, held in the right way and exchanged between the right people. This means that we must ask the question – Who needs to know what? – which, as you see, is the title of this block.

Unit 22 *Sharing Knowledge*, looks first at what people need to know about the services they might want to use and at how service providers can make this knowledge available to them. It then switches to looking at how service users can become sufficiently 'in the know' to be involved in shaping services to make them responsive to users' needs. Unit 23 *Confidentiality: Managing Personal Information*, discusses what care service providers need to know about the people who use their services; what records need to be kept and why; how and where they should be stored; and who should be allowed access to them, bearing in mind people's rights to confidentiality. Unit 24 *Accountability*, examines the growing pressures on care providers to be able to account for the standards of services they provide, particularly when things go wrong. It shows the crucial role of written down procedures, effective record keeping and clear lines of reporting, in keeping service users, carers and service managers in the know about what ought to happen and what actually happens. Finally Unit 25 *Letting the Right People Know*, focuses on skills in presenting information that is appropriate to the circumstances and on practical decision making about passing on confidential information.

Unit 22
Sharing Knowledge

Originally prepared for the course team by Roger Gomm

Substantially redeveloped by Marion Reichart and Danielle Turney

---

While you are working on Unit 22, you will need:

- Offprints Book
- Care Systems and Structures
- Unit 13
- Audio Cassette 6, side 2

Contents

Introduction

This unit is about making services more accessible to people. One of the main ways this can be done is by providing them with information about what is available and how it works. But, as we said in the introduction to the block, 'information' by itself is not enough. People need particular kinds of information, and they need it in an accessible form, and available at the right time. So here, we start to look at the issues involved in sharing information effectively. We also look at how the people who use services can be more fully involved in the design, management and evaluation of the services they use. In this respect this unit picks up and discusses issues you considered in Unit 10, but emphasises the important role that sharing information plays in making services more accessible and in the planning of services.

Increasing both accessibility and user involvement has been something that:

- organised groups of service users have campaigned for
- central government has attempted to impose on health and social services
- health and social care providers have attempted to implement in their own services.

How far such initiatives have been successful is another matter.

Section 1 sets the scene. It considers the large number of very diverse agencies in the health and social care field in any major area of population. It points out how difficult it can be for would-be service users to find out about the existence of these agencies, let alone what they do and whether they are relevant to them. Practitioners in health and social care often have similar difficulties and this limits their ability to give information or advice to clients.

If people are to access services they need information to do it

If people are to access services they need information. But service providers sometimes struggle to find the best way to share information about their services with potential users and they, in turn, can find it difficult to find and then make use of relevant information. Section 2 looks in more detail at why this situation occurs and what can be done to make access to information easier.

We started by noting that service provision in any given area will be both complex and diverse. But the complexity and diversity of services is not just a problem of information. It is also a problem of co-ordination. How can the diverse services in a local area co-ordinate their activities one with another? And how can local people, the users of those services, have a say in what happens in their area? Section 3 looks at some answers to these questions. The diversity and complexity of services requires service users to develop skills in seeking information, as well as skills in the sharing of information, planning of services and working in partnership. To develop these skills they need opportunities to become involved.

Section 4 looks at one way this can happen – through self-advocacy. It considers the skills of self-advocacy, using an audio cassette featuring people with learning difficulties at Leavesden Hospital who formed a self-advocacy group. It also considers the differences between advocacy, which you read about in Unit 10, and self-advocacy.

Core questions

- Who needs to know what about services? Where can information be found?

- Why can it be difficult to find out about services? And what measures can be taken to improve the quality and dissemination of information about services?

- How can service users be more fully involved in the planning, management and evaluation of the services they use?

- What skills and what support do service users need in order to be more fully involved?

Section 1
Finding out about services

This section looks at information about services as a two-way process. Service users need to know what services are available to them. And people who plan and provide services need to know what services are required in their area, and by whom.

To start thinking about these issues, we will go back to Mandy Brown and her young son Sean. They were the lone-parent family you met in Unit 13. Mandy did not know anyone else in the area she had recently moved in to; she was unemployed and was going for a part-time job at a factory. A major worry was that her flat was damp and that Sean had severe asthma. In that unit you practised the skills of assessing their needs, and considered what kinds of services might satisfy these needs. You saw how difficult it was at times for Mandy to find out what she needed to know.

The services were scattered around different agencies, and sometimes in different departments in the same agency. Offprint 27, 'Services which might be relevant to the needs of Mandy and Sean Brown', gives a list of the kinds of services that *might* be relevant to Mandy and Sean in a typical English town. Much the same list could be produced for urban areas in Wales, Scotland or Northern Ireland, though some of the agencies would have different names. Find Offprint 27 now and look at it. It will be useful to have this Offprint to hand throughout this unit. We shall also make use of the Care Systems and Structures booklet.

Activity 1   **Re-visiting Offprint 27 'Services which might be relevant to the needs of Mandy and Sean Brown'**

Allow about 5 minute   Look back over pages 154-6 of Unit 13 and remind yourself of Mandy and Sean's situation. Then look again at the range of services in Offprint 27. What do you think Mandy's reaction would be if she was given this list? Would it be easy for Mandy to find out which services were appropriate for her and how to access them?

Comment   I guess Mandy might feel overwhelmed by a list like this one. Where should she begin?

Of course, only some of the services listed would turn out to be appropriate for Mandy and Sean. Equally, she and he would only be eligible for some of them. Would social services, for example, supply services to Sean?

Eligibility

Different services will operate with different eligibility criteria. For example, the Children Act 1989 talks in terms of children who are 'in need'.

Section 17(10) Children Act 1989 defines a child 'in need' as follows:

(a)   he is unlikely to maintain ... a reasonable standard of health or development without the provision for him of services by a local authority

(b)   his health or development is likely to be significantly impaired, or further impaired, without the provision for him of such services; or

(c)   he is disabled.

If the social services department (SSD) classified Sean as 'disabled' due to his severe asthma, he could become eligible for services under Section 17(10) of the Children Act 1989. But if Sean were seen merely as a poor child he would not be eligible on this ground alone, unless his health or development were likely to be 'significantly impaired'. So if Mandy needed financial support, it's likely that she would have to look elsewhere - but where? Without knowing details about all the agencies on the list it is impossible to decide whether they are worth approaching: impossible for you; impossible for Mandy and very difficult for any health or care practitioner trying to help her to access and use the services needed. Remember that this is just a list for Mandy and Sean. The lists for the other people you encountered in Unit 13 would be different.

1.1   Who needs to know what about services?

People need information about services for different reasons. Someone like Mandy, for example, needs information as a potential service user herself and she also needs information as a carer for her son. But all the people Mandy met in the video needed information too. In this section, we look at the different information needs that individuals can have. To get an idea of the range of people who need information, and the kind of information they need, we now leave Mandy and instead visit the Grove Health Centre. The Grove Health Centre is fictional, but based upon real people and real issues. Through the experiences of the different people associated with the Centre, we shall explore some of the difficulties of supplying the right kind of information, at the right time and in the right format to the people who need it.

The Grove Health Centre

The Grove Health Centre is in a quiet residential area, on the edge of a large housing estate in an outer London borough. There are 3 GPs, a Practice Nurse, and a full-time receptionist. A part-time counsellor runs a number of groups, and a dietician does a weekly clinic. One of the consulting rooms is used by a variety of local therapists including an acupuncturist and an osteopath. In addition, there is a weekly baby clinic, and a twice-weekly 'surgery' offered by one of the social workers from the local authority Adult Disability Team. Workers at the Grove HC have links with, and make referrals to, a number of local organisations. One of these is the Narcotics Information and Advice Service (NIAS), a local 'street' drugs agency that offers information and counselling to people who are using drugs and may have problems in connection with their habit.

Here are some people connected to the Grove Health Centre:

- One of the three GPs of the Grove Health Centre is Dr. June Li (aged 46). Of Chinese origin she speaks Cantonese and English. She is single and has recently become an informal carer for her father, Mr. Thomas Li, aged 80.

    He speaks mainly Cantonese and has a small network of friends. Dr. Li has knowledge of both traditional Chinese Medicine and western medical practice. She has a particular interest in 'whole-person' approaches to health and disease and would like to focus attention on preventable ill health conditions.

- Beverley Jackson (aged 52) white English. She is a home care worker employed by Care Matters, and looks after clients living in their own homes, like Arthur Durrant. She speaks English and uses Makaton. Beverley is interested in furthering her career but is unsure which direction to take.

- Michelle McDonald (aged 24), white Scottish. She is currently looking for part-time work. Michelle is a heroin user and has referred herself to a local 'street' drug agency, the Narcotics Information and Advice Service (NIAS). Michelle has a daughter, Sarah, who is 18 months old. Michelle and Sarah only moved into the area recently. Her parents and other family are all in Scotland and she has little contact with them. Michelle has no accommodation of her own and is 'in priority need' for housing under the Housing Act 1996 since she is looking after a young child.

- Wayne Morgan (aged 28) white English. Wayne is also a client of NIAS and the local authority drug problem team. He is a heavy user of amphetamine sulphate ('speed') which causes him to behave in ways that other people find bizarre. He is currently unemployed but at times finds casual work. He has no fixed address and often sleeps rough, though at the moment he is staying with his mother.

- Dev Sharma (aged 40) is Asian British and speaks Hindi, English and some Punjabi. He is married to Gita and they have three children; their middle daughter, Kulvinder (aged 10) has cerebral palsy. Dev's main occupation is as a qualified social worker with the local authority disability team.

- Pat Walsh (aged 48) is black British with African-Caribbean family ties and speaks English and French. She is married. Recently, her husband was diagnosed with a kidney disease. Pat works four days per week as the receptionist at the Grove Health Centre and has lived in the area all her life. She volunteers at the local 'street' drug agency Narcotics Information and Advice Services (NIAS).

Each of the people introduced above will have a variety of information needs. For example, if we think about Dr Li: as a GP, Dr. Li needs to know what services are available at the Grove Health Centre and in her local area. She needs to know where to refer her patients for specialist treatment and how to get supplies of certain vaccines; she also needs to know how to refer patients on for other services, for example home care, occupational therapy etc.

As she is thinking of targeting 'preventable' diseases, in particular those related to high blood pressure and certain heart conditions, she needs to know the extent of this problem in her area, what other agencies are trying to do about it, and what local people would expect. She also needs to know how much money she has available to spend on it and whether there are any more pressing health issues that need to be tackled.

But in addition to all the information she needs to fulfil her role as a doctor, Dr Li also needs to know about services in relation to her informal caring role for her father. She may want to find out what domiciliary services are available, and whether home care support that is available will respect Chinese cultural traditions and Mr. Li's preferences.

Pat Walsh, the receptionist at Grove Health Centre, may be asked by waiting patients about all kinds of things, not just about the services offered within the practice. So she needs to know a lot, for example about local mother and toddler groups, where to go for childcare, how to contact an informal carer support network, how to find the address for an organisation like Arthritis Care or other agencies. When making appointments for patients, she needs to know the availability of each of the three general practitioners and she needs basic information about the patients, such as their full name and address. Sometimes, Pat is asked to make an urgent appointment and in order to decide how to deal with this she needs information from the patient about symptoms and circumstances.

As a volunteer at NIAS, Pat needs to know what services her agency can offer, and what services are provided by other agencies. She needs to have up-to-date information about such additional agencies as careers services, family planning or citizens advice. Pat also needs to know what is expected of her as a volunteer, what tasks she is to perform and whether or not she can claim expenses for some of her activities. Outside work, though, she also needs to know about the services offered by the renal unit that her husband attends, how to get in touch with the doctors there, how she and her husband can manage his illness effectively, and so on. Also, when she gets a bit of free time, Pat likes to attend a yoga class, so she has been trying to find out what classes are organised in her local area.

Michelle McDonald wants to know about the services offered by local drugs agencies. She has heard about NIAS but needs to find out what the agency offers, its opening hours and availability of staff and volunteers, etc. Michelle needs help with finding a part-time job and therefore also wants to know whether NIAS offers careers advice or similar services or whether she will have to go elsewhere. As the mother of a small child, she also requires information about services for her daughter; this could include details of the baby clinics, local play facilities, a list of registered child-minders or nurseries etc.

<table>
<tr><td>Activity 2</td><td>**Your information needs**</td></tr>
</table>

Activity 2   **Your information needs**

Allow about 5 minutes   Having read about the different sorts of information needs that Dr Li, Pat Walsh and Michelle McDonald have, spend a few minutes thinking about the range of information that **you** need in the course of an average week. Think about the different roles you occupy, personally and professionally, and jot down the sorts of information you need in these different capacities.

Comment   There is no specific comment on this activity, but we would guess that the list you come up with will be every bit as varied - and complicated - as the ones set out above!

In any one area, there will be a large number of diverse agencies in the health and social care field; in our example, this includes the Grove Health Centre, the voluntary street drug agency NIAS, the private provider of care *Care Matters,* and statutory social services. Finding out about what services might be appropriate, whether or not one is entitled to use such a service and where else to go if the particular service is not available can be difficult. Some services can be accessed only by referral from a doctor, a social worker or some other practitioner. Unit 10 discussed 'gate-keeping' in primary health care and the fact that GPs control access to a range of services. The example of Mandy and Sean in Activity 1 illustrated how children may be entitled to help from social services. But in order to use any service, you first need to know that it exists. The next section looks at how to promote awareness of a service.

1.2   Where can information be found?

Dr. June Li has only recently joined the Grove Health Centre practice. She is concerned with promoting the services available to patients and has been asked to think about advertising what the Grove Health Centre has to offer.

Activity 3   **Promoting a service**

Allow about 15 minutes   Read the scenario of 'Dr Li's dilemma'.

Dr Li's dilemma

Dr. June Li has the task of advertising the services of the Grove Health Centre. In addition to the usual services offered by a GP practice, Dr. Li is interested in reducing stress-induced health conditions. She thinks an increase in levels of participation in the 'stress-busters' programme might make a significant difference. Stress-busters is a series of linked programmes, involving a health check, an initial assessment by the practice nurse, advice and support from a dietician, a lifestyle review, and weekly relaxation classes. The programme might include support for a particular stressful event, such as bereavement counselling, a course of acupuncture or the prescription of relevant medication. Dr. Li was thinking about what *media* she could use to promote the service (pamphlets, newspaper advertisements and so on) and how she could *target* the information – whom she would try to reach. Since she had only a limited budget available, she decided to have a leaflet designed and distributed 5,000 copies at the surgery, the local library, two main shopping centres and the post office. However, after three weeks the Grove Health Centre had only seven enquiries asking for details of the 'stress busting' programme.

Dr Li was surprised by this, and wondered why she had received so few enquiries. Her first thoughts were that either the information she sent out was somehow wrong for the task, or it was the right information, but somehow failed to reach the right people.

Reflecting further on her experience, Dr Li came up with a number of key questions to help her address these two points:

Who do I want to see this information? Who makes up the 'target group'?

What do I need to tell them?

How can I best convey that information? That is, what media can I use?

Where shall I distribute the information?

If you were Dr Li, how would you start to answer these questions?

Comment   The kinds of media you might have considered include: leaflets, posters and, if you weren't counting the cost, local newspaper, radio and television advertisements. For example, Dr. Li might appear during morning TV's 'doc spot' at her local television or radio station. Or she might have a pamphlet designed showing people of all ages and backgrounds in business dress, casual wear or boiler suits to show that stress can affect anyone. On the other hand, she might go for a hard-hitting poster campaign showing loved-ones at the hospital bed of a patient admitted with a heart attack. Or she might have thought of teaming-up with an agency promoting healthy living, such as the British Heart Foundation. In choosing between these or various other possibilities, the first question to ask is 'Who are we targeting?' You might, for example, attempt to inform the kinds of people who would use the service, for example 'rushed-off their feet business people'. Or you might target the kinds of people or agencies who would be in a position to pass on the information, such as social workers, health visitors, disablement advisers, Citizens Advice Bureaux, and so on.

A further question is 'Where shall we distribute the information?' You may have devised a very effective leaflet, but it will be no use if it is not distributed to the 'right' outlets. You could start by targeting venues where potential service users gather: Grove Health Centre's own waiting rooms, for example. The problem, however, is that this would target only those patients who are already attending the GP surgery. Others who might benefit will be missed. And it may be those very people – the ones who are too busy to come to the surgery in the first place – who would most benefit from reducing their stress levels. Another approach would be to distribute information leaflets at local post offices or shopping centres where they can be seen by a much larger number of people. The problem then is whether people doing their weekly shopping or queueing at the Post Office are interested in picking up and reading a leaflet about health matters. People doing this for real often find they have a choice between blanketing an area with publicity, the vast majority of it reaching people who don't need it, or closely targeting the most obvious points of contact, and then running the risk that some potential users – probably the most needy – won't have such a contact point. Doing both takes more time and more money.

For your own area you probably know the kinds of places where information of this kind tends to accumulate: in pamphlet racks and on notice boards in libraries, doctors' surgeries, Citizens Advice Bureaux, or in the council rent office.

This is the right shelf – it says large print books for short-sighted readers!

In such places you can often find information about 50 or more services. But how many people actually take the information away? Of those, how many read it? And of those, how many act on it? Research from the commercial world is not very encouraging. For commercial flyers and pamphlets, for example, it is generally reckoned that there is one sale for every 3,000 pamphlets distributed (MacIntosh, 1987). (Looking at it from this point of view, seven enquiries for 5,000 'stress-busters' leaflets is a good up-take.) And this refers to advertising, frequently called 'junk mail', carefully targeted according to age, income group and information about purchasing habits, often with incentives such as prize draws and free gifts. When did your social services department last offer you a chance to win a free holiday?

The parallel with commercial advertising is informative. Promotional literature distributed for commercial purposes is usually produced on a generous budget, by people who are expert in researching the market and discovering the kinds of messages that are most likely to grab the consumer's interest and provoke them to action. Apart from nationally mounted health promotion campaigns – about, for example, smoking or HIV – few organisations in the health and social care field can match this. And the experience of health education campaigns is that while they are often effective in changing what people *know*, they are much less effective in changing what people *do* (Whitehead, 1989).

Key points

- Both service users and service providers may need information about a wide range of services.

- It is often difficult to find out about the services that are available in a particular area.

- Materials alone, such as leaflets, posters and advertisements are relatively ineffectual in encouraging people to do things.

Section 2

Why can it be difficult to find out about services? Barriers to information

However large the budget available or the methods chosen to distribute information, it is important that information about health and social care services directed at possible users is well designed. This section introduces criteria of 'good design' and discusses scenarios based on the Grove Health Centre to explore their meaning.

2.1 Designing for your audiences

Section 1 considered the large number of very diverse health and social care agencies that may be found in any particular area of population and the information needs that arise for potential service users and practitioners. This section is concerned with how to reach the person for whom information is intended by ensuring good design. By 'good design' we mean that information should:

- be designed for a diverse range of people who are likely to be using the services

- answer the questions they want answered

- use language and formats they can understand

- be available at the time when it is needed.

The illustration overleaf gives you an example of picture-supported information produced by people with learning difficulties, for people with learning difficulties. Lots of people without learning difficulties might also find this easier to understand than most 'official' communications. So the picture support makes the information accessible to a wider audience, by including people both with and without learning difficulties.

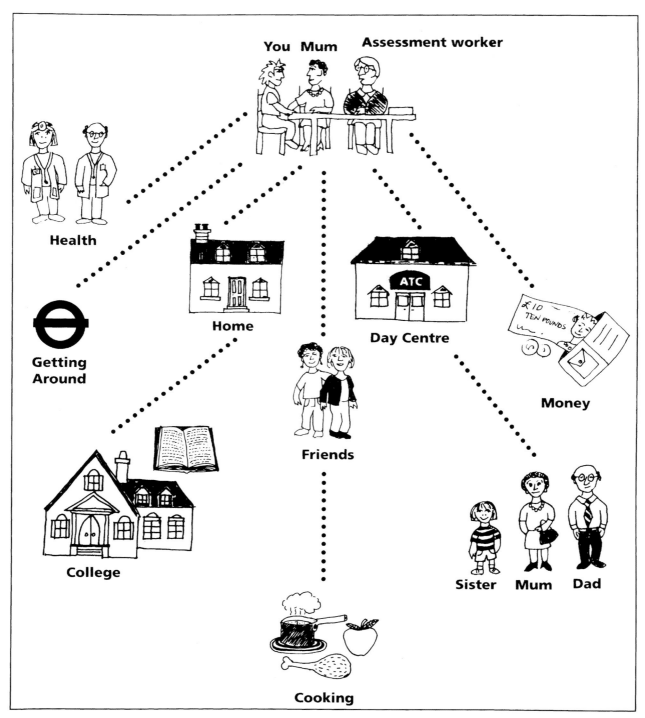

You Mum   Assessment worker

Health

Getting Around

Home

ATC

Day Centre

Money

College

Friends

Sister   Mum   Dad

Cooking

People First, an organisation of people with learning difficulties, has been very successful in making information easier to understand

Making information available in minority languages may be another reflection of good design as it, too, is a way of increasing access. In Activity 3 you might have thought that one reason for the low uptake of information on 'stress-busting' was the fact that the leaflet apparently was only available in English. The Grove Health Centre, however, serves a large Bangladeshi community and a smaller Chinese community as well as a sizeable group of Turkish Kurdish refugees. Community languages and cultural diversity raise issues of 'good design' and appropriate information. As the Grove Health Centre is within the Greater London Area, it could call upon the Asian Health Agency for the London Boroughs (TAHA) for advice. TAHA aims to serve the different but equal needs within diverse communities and provides a range of services, including interpreting. However, since TAHA focuses on Asian health needs the Grove Health Centre would still need to find appropriate language support services for its Chinese and Turkish Kurdish patients.

The Disability Discrimination Act 1995 has introduced a duty on service providers to consider the rights of equal access of disabled people. In order to avoid discriminating against disabled people when designing information, Dr. Li would have to think about making information about services available in alternative media, such as large print, information in Braille and on tape. In thinking about people with learning difficulties, for example, the NHS Executive has produced a document aimed at promoting good practice (Lindsey and Russell, 1999, p. 3) which Dr Li could use. The booklet is called 'Once A Day' because one or more people with learning disabilities are likely to be in contact with a primary health care trust in any one day. Grove Health Centre is one of three GP practices within a primary care trust (see Figure 1) and would expect a proportion of its patients to be people with learning difficulties. Usually a general practitioner with a list of 2,000 patients will have about 40 patients with learning difficulties, although there is considerable local variation. Of these 40 patients about eight will have severe learning disabilities (Lindsey and Russell, 1999, p. 3). It is recognised that people with learning difficulties from minority ethnic groups receive less help from all agencies, including health services, so particular efforts are needed to reach this group of service users. The extension of the Race Relations Act has placed duties on all public services to consider and actively promote inclusion of all ethnic groups. This requires positive steps to be taken and could start with the design of information.

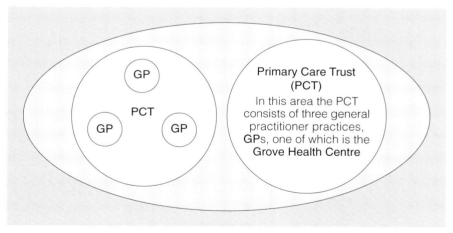

Figure 1 Grove Health Centre as part of a primary care trust

Some agencies have made great strides in producing information that is accessible and informative, and respects people's beliefs and preferences (Wiltshire Social Services, 1993; Moffatt, 1993; University of Warwick, 1993). Well-designed information allows service users to find things out for themselves rather than having to rely on someone else. So, alternative formats for information enable people to develop their own potential, rather than being made dependent on others.

There is no doubt that the user-friendliness of literature produced by health and care agencies has improved greatly since the 1980s. Some of this is due to the impact of the Disability Discrimination Act 1995 and the influence of the Campaign for Plain English (Cutts and Maher, 1980), now widely consulted by agencies such as the Benefits Agency and the

Inland Revenue, as well as by several NHS trusts. As you saw above, the user-led organisations, such as People First and TAHA have also played a part in making information more accessible (People First, 1994).

The Royal National Institute for the Blind (RNIB) has conducted research into accessibility of health service information for blind and partially-sighted people. They suggest that:

- Patient information leaflets, medicine labels and instructions, and appointment letters should all be available to each patient in their preferred "format" - in large clear type, on disc, on tape or in Braille

- Telephone help-lines - with the number in large, clear print on labels or in patient information leaflets - can give patients details of side effects and dosages

- Confidential medical results or treatment options can be given in person over the telephone

- Braille labelling should be available on all over-the-counter medicines (something that the Co-op have now introduced)

- NHS trusts should have clear policies and plans to ensure information is accessible to all patients.

Agencies can work together to promote good practice. In Northern Ireland, for example, RNIB and RNID have worked together to help GP practices improve their service to patients with sight or hearing problems

However, this is still not common practice. One of the reasons for this might be that service providers fail to recognise diversity. In addition, there may be attitudinal barriers to good practice that are expressed in different ways:

- lack of resources ('our budget does not stretch to providing Braille')

- lack of training or expertise ('we don't speak Urdu or use sign language') and

- lack of specialist equipment ('we don't have a transcription service available').

For example, Dr. Li might be wondering how far her budget would spread if she had to translate and transcribe all Grove Health Centre service information. She may feel it costly to bring in community language or sign language interpreters. She might think about the other things that money could be spent on. However, if Dr Li spends the money she does have available on pamphlets and advertising, but only reaches a limited proportion of members of the community who find it useful, then not all her money is spent wisely.

Differences in cultural and language background, and attitudes towards diversity or disability are not the only factors playing a role in whether or not the message reaches its intended audience. Other factors include differences in education or occupational background.

Kulvinder Sharma

Kulvinder is about to move up to secondary school. She has cerebral palsy which affects her speech, movement and co-ordination. However, she is doing well at the small local primary school; her friends soon get used to her slower speech and their ears become 'trained' enabling them to understand what Kulvinder is saying. They like hanging out with her, and say she is fun to be with and has a wicked sense of humour. The nearest secondary school is housed on two floors and has a large, secluded playground. The Sharma family is waiting for an assessment to see if Kulvinder will be able to go there. Dev Sharma might say:

'Wading through assessment forms is no problem for me. I am used to this from my work. I have a fair understanding of what services are on offer. I know, for example, about the Children Act 1989 and Section 17 assistance. This can give me help with my daughter, Kulvinder. However, the new Special Educational Needs and Disability Act 2001 is less familiar to me. I need to find out more about it and whether it will help my daughter to attend the local mainstream school. She wants to stay with her friends, and we don't want her to go to the special school.'

Since Dev Sharma is employed as a social worker, the Sharma family are likely to be very familiar with some aspects of service information. In particular, they may be familiar with some of the professional jargon and specialised language, and have knowledge of some social services and health service systems. They may also be less frightened of 'professionals' who come to visit their home, and feel more comfortable with relevant forms and paperwork. However, not many of Dr Li's patients will have this kind of 'inside' knowledge and will not find it easy to wade through quantities of often quite complicated information.

As we have seen in this section, information needs to be designed to be accessible to people with a range of communication needs, and failure to consider design can present a serious barrier to access. So service providers need to make sure that their information is as clear and straightforward as possible and is available in the format the service user finds most helpful.

Key point

- Information telling people directly about services needs to be well designed and to answer the questions they want answered in a language and format they can use.

2.2 Do they mean me?

Service users need to identify with the information that is being presented. They need to feel it is meant for them and is immediately relevant to their situation, otherwise, no matter how much information is given out, it is wasted. A further barrier to information, therefore, may lie in the way people respond to it.

Assuming that people actually get the information (which is the first hurdle) and would benefit from the service (which is the second), they tend to respond only if *at the time* it is immediately relevant to them. The pamphlet advertising Grove Health Centre's 'stress busting' programme carries a 'one-shot' message. If people don't connect with the message immediately, they tend to ignore it. Stress busting? No, this doesn't concern me. And even if they read it, they tend to forget it quickly. This is one of the reasons for the recent popularity of distributing calendars with information about services round the edges. At least they might stay on the wall for 12 months and remind you about the services advertised. Commercial advertisers, too, present the same message hour after hour and day after day on commercial radio and television, to try and keep their name and product in your mind.

Many of the people health and social care services want to reach are upset, confused, depressed, alienated or otherwise not very responsive. This makes it more challenging to design information, and channels of information, which would get through to them. People need to recognise themselves in a particular message and say 'yes, that's me' (Althuser, 1971). Vulnerable people in particular may need support in paying attention to and recognising the relevance of information that comes their way.

Processes involved in labelling are another potential barrier. In Unit 1 you discussed different situations in which informal carers found themselves. One problem in accessing relevant services might have been their reluctance to accept the label 'informal carer'. Any service offered, for example, to enable informal carers to continue in their role would not reach the intended audience if they did not recognise that they *were* the audience, or did not accept that particular 'label' for themselves.

Labelling emerged as an issue in a study by the Joseph Rowntree Foundation (Jones *et al.*, 2002). Researchers were interested in young people with caring responsibilities in black families, and found that the label 'carer' was not one that the young people used about themselves; nor did it bring any positive benefits to them:

A study called **'Invisible Families: The Strengths and Needs of Black Families in which Young People have Caring Responsibilities'** for the Joseph Rowntree Foundation found that:

> *'Young people did not identify with the term 'carer'. This categorisation made no positive difference to the support they or their families received, and it made them feel different from other people.'*

(*Jones* et al., 2002)

That study also identified another and rather different problem - the attitude of the agency. The researchers noted that 'Agencies did not routinely gather information on young people with caring responsibilities and professionals' awareness of the issues was very low.'

The study illustrates two sets of barriers to information, one from the service user's point of view ('do they mean me?') and the other from the agency perspective (the attitude that there is no need to collate information about young carers). A different aspect of the 'do they mean me?' problem is explored by Lazarsfeld *et al.*, (1944). They argue that

people rarely respond to promotional material without discussing this with other people. This is illustrated by Michelle's dilemma.

Michelle McDonald's dilemma

At the baby clinic at the Grove Health Centre, Michelle's GP, Dr.Li, noticed how tired and lethargic Michelle was and asked how well she slept at night, and whether the baby kept her awake. Michelle was very suspicious and worried that her skills as a mother might be questioned. She was also keen to hide the fact that she was a heroin user, but to no avail. Dr Li observed evidence of drug use and talked to Michelle about the Narcotics Information and Advice Service (NIAS). She wrote the address and telephone number on a piece of paper and handed this to Michelle. The next day the piece of paper was lost in the washing, and Michelle did not seek help from NIAS.

Two weeks later, Michelle met Wayne Morgan for the first time. They became friends, and Wayne told Michelle how useful he found the services of NIAS and how understanding volunteers like Pat were. Another week after that, Michelle referred herself to NIAS.

NIAS is a 'street' drug agency, which means that people can refer themselves to it directly, by walking through the door or by telephone. It also accepts referrals from the GPs at the Grove Health Centre as long as the person concerned has given consent and agrees to be dealt with by NIAS. When Michelle was told about NIAS by her GP, she did not take any action as a result of having obtained information. It was not until she became friends with Wayne and, having heard his experience of attending NIAS, became so interested in what they had to offer that she decided to go along too.

People need to be able to imagine themselves using a service

People need to be able to imagine themselves using a service, as Michelle was able to when she saw that she was in a similar situation to Wayne's. In smaller, more close-knit communities in the past, services may not have been very extensive, but there was always someone who knew what was available at the Miners' Welfare, or the infant welfare clinic, or which dentist inflicted most pain, and which doctor was prepared to waive his fees. There are still communities like this, but many people live outside such networks of information. There is a 'first step' problem here for services that people access themselves. Not many people take the first step unaided.

Serena, who is a carers' support worker, says:

> It can take literally years to persuade someone to come to a support group meeting, and work by me and the CPN [community psychiatric nurse] and the practice nurse, and the doctor and so on. Even if we can arrange for the care of the person [being looked after] then I nearly always have myself to bring the carer to the group. Unless, that is, they are introduced by a friend. Then no problem. And, of course, once they have made the first step then they've got some other people they can go to other things with.

Maureen, who organises monthly outings for older people, says:

> The average length of time it takes is three months. That's two offers refused and the third accepted. But sometimes it can be several years. But then of course it's 'When's the next one?' and it's difficult to strike a balance between giving places to satisfied customers and holding places open for newcomers. Or it's 'Can my friend come?' Or 'I'll only come if my friend comes'. Unfortunately some of the friends aren't disabled or housebound so they're not strictly eligible.

The same groups of friends can often be found using a variety of facilities (Brighton Polytechnic, 1992). They learn about them from each other, just as Michelle learned from Wayne. They value each other's support and company in attending them. In contrast, people who don't have the support of a network often use no such services at all.

All this points to the importance of social networks in carrying information about services and in supporting people to use them (Gottlieb, 1981). In turn it suggests the importance in health and social care of helping people to develop their networks of contacts, and of using the kinds of community development and network-building strategies discussed in Unit 12. Put another way, you can't build communities by showering people with leaflets. It is where there is no community that people are least likely to respond to such information.

Key points

- People need to imagine themselves as using a particular service and need to identify with its label in order to respond to information.

- People are more likely to respond to information if it comes from people they know, and if they have their encouragement in accessing services.

Section 3
Sharing knowledge

The unit so far has been about the information needed to access services. The remainder of the unit will be about the information needed to improve the co-ordination of services and to enable those who use services to play a greater part in determining the way they operate. These two issues are closely connected.

 Look again at Offprint 27, the list of services that might be relevant to Mandy and Sean. There are three different statutory and a range of independent service providers listed. This suggests a problem of co-ordination. Most of the agencies listed are autonomous, sometimes to a considerable degree. They have their own ways of managing their affairs, their own philosophies, their own ways of setting priorities, and their own systems for planning their activities. Put simply, the list gives you a glimpse of a system of health and social care that is very poorly co-ordinated. It is hardly a 'system' at all insofar as the term 'system' implies co-ordination. Information needs to be shared between service providers in order to offer a co-ordinated response to service need.

 The diagrams in Care Systems and Structures were designed to cover only those services that are most obviously 'health' and 'social care' services. But, thinking of Mandy and Sean again, there are many agencies that fall outside this narrow definition, which are none the less relevant to their health and welfare. These are listed in the third column of Offprint 27. For example, housing seems to be more important for Sean's health than anything provided through the 'health service'. Income from the Benefits Agency is perhaps currently the most important basis for their health and welfare. The Child Support Agency is likely to enter Mandy's life soon if it has not done so already. Education and training might well improve her prospects. Mandy is likely to be a candidate for schemes such as the Welfare to Work programme, which will provide her with childcare while she works or trains. Some education and training providers offer counselling for personal problems, some provide accommodation, and some in the private sector even provide some health care for trainees.

So health and social care needs are met not only by what are usually thought of as 'health' and/or 'social care' agencies. In fact, for a very large percentage of the population, the most important services sustaining their health and social welfare lie outside the orbit of the NHS and the social services departments. The important point here is that when it comes to planning the health and care services for a local area, a wide range of agencies needs to be involved. If you wanted to convene a meeting to review and make recommendations about services for, say, lone-parent families in an area, you would probably want to invite representatives from all the agencies listed in Offprint 27. But some lone-parent families have members with disabilities, some include members with mental health problems, some are from minority ethnic backgrounds, some include members who have broken the law or have problems with illicit drugs or alcohol. You can see that the set of organisations you might consider inviting to your meeting is growing larger. You would need a spacious venue to include them all.

3.1 Having a voice in planning

The NHS and Community Care Act 1990 imposed a legal duty on local authority social services and social work authorities to draw up and annually review plans for the *social care* aspects of community care – so-called 'community care plans'. The health and social services boards in Northern Ireland were given similar responsibilities. They required every social services department to publish a plan for community care services in its area. The idea behind this legal requirement was that local authorities should provide services that are actually needed by its population and not plan services first and then see who wants them.

Although this legal duty under the 1990 Act was removed in April 2002, it is likely that alternative arrangements will be brought in to ensure that adequate information is made available to those who need it. And removing the duty to produce a community care plan is clearly not going to affect the need for service planning to continue, within local authorities.

With so many different agencies involved covering large geographical areas planning for appropriate services is no easy task. None the less, in the abstract the planning process is easy enough to understand. One way of looking at it is in terms of Figure 2.

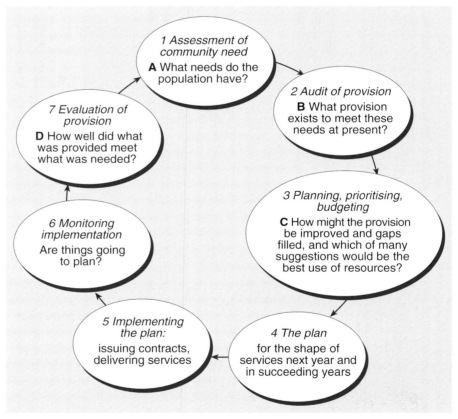

Figure 2 The planning process in health and social care

In looking at Figure 2, note that 'planning' is not just something that happens in advance and then stops. It should be something that goes on all the time, as information becomes available through the experience of delivering services.

The important questions for planning are relatively simple to ask. What needs do the population have? Look at the questions in Figure 2:

- What provisions already exist to meet these needs?
- Where are the gaps and how might they be filled?
- What is the plan for the next year and the next five years?
- Are things going to plan?
- How well are services meeting the needs?

The answers, however, are not straightforward. The different people connected with the Grove Health Centre, for example, may all have different ideas about what service should be prioritised over the next year. Furthermore, it is important to appreciate the scale and the complexity of this planning. The following example usefully illustrates this point; though it refers to the planning that took place within the community care planning system that has now been phased out, it does give a good sense of the complexity and scale of this kind of locality planning.

> The community care plan for the county of Hertfordshire covers a population of just over a million people, and refers to social services expenditure of around £195 million (1997/98). The lead agency for community care planning is the county council as a social services authority. But the plan has to be drawn up in consultation with the county's own education, probation, police and trading standards authorities, two health authorities, about 125 general practices, seven NHS trusts, eight district councils, which are the housing, environmental health and public transport authorities, and 12 housing associations, which provide special needs housing. At a rough estimate there are around 200 residential and nursing homes that are supposed to be consulted and about 7,000 voluntary sector organisations in the health and social care field. Planning for health care involves much the same agencies, but much more money.

Planning, then, is clearly a difficult and complicated task. So is there any scope for members of the public to be involved? Apart from planning committees which meet on a regular basis at town halls or civic centres, some areas consult the 'general public' by using social survey techniques – questionnaires administered to representative samples of the general public (Bowling, 1993). Other areas use focus groups or 'citizen juries' (Bromley Health, 1995; Brindle, 1995; Ogden, 1996). Focus groups are small groups of people chosen to represent the different kinds of individuals in the area. Beverley Jackson has been active in one of these groups, representing a particular section of the population locally, namely those who work in private care services. She has been asked to choose between different options for the development of health and social care services. Although the decisions of her focus group are not the last word on what is actually planned for, their views will be fed in to the planning process. In yet other areas the 'general public' doesn't seem to be consulted at all.

To produce the kind of plan discussed above, it is necessary to break the process down into manageable pieces. First, not everyone can be consulted, so it is necessary to create representative structures: for example, one GP may represent all the practices in an area, or a representative of a federation of residential homes may represent all of these, or there may be an electoral system through which the large number of voluntary groups elect people to represent the voluntary sector as a whole. Second, planning is often done separately for different service user groups – for older people, people with physical difficulties, children and families, people with mental health problems, and so on. And, third, it is done by breaking down large areas into smaller planning localities. This has the advantage of allowing planning to be sensitive to the particular needs of different localities and to increase the numbers of people and agencies that can be involved in the process.

Key points

- Local authorities and health authorities had a legal obligation to draw up and annually review a community care plan. This duty was removed in April 2002, and it is not clear yet what might replace it. However, it is clear that planning will have to continue at this level, involving both these authorities and an increasing range of local agencies.

- Authorities have a duty to provide services that are actually needed by their populations and not plan services first, then see who wants them.

- Knowledge about what and how to provide services comes from service providers. To complete the planning process the views of service users are required.

Section 4
Self-advocacy: challenging professional perspectives

The key points that ended Section 3 made it clear that service users have a crucial role to play in the planning process. But it may be very difficult for people to get involved or to feel that they have the skills to make a proper contribution. So how can their views best be heard? In Unit 10 you read about advocacy. Most of the comments there concerned advocating for individuals, with the advocate making a case on behalf of a would-be service user to help them get the best possible deal from services. This section, however, is about *self-advocacy*. So it is necessary to consider what the differences are between the two practices.

4.1 Advocacy and self-advocacy

The movement towards self-advocacy was one of the most important developments in health and social care in the 1980s and particularly in the 1990s (Robson, 1987; Crawley, 1988; Beresford and Campbell, 1990; Campbell, 1996). It has taken place across North America, New Zealand, Australia and Europe with regard to people who have physical impairments; people with communicative difficulties, such as impaired vision or hearing; people regarded as having learning difficulties or as being mentally ill; and among older people more generally. Self-advocacy groups have taken considerable inspiration from the civil rights movements among black people, from feminism and from the gay and lesbian movement. As in these movements, the major demand is to be treated as people with the same rights as other citizens, including the right to self-determination. This includes the right to define one's own needs, rather than to have them defined by others, and may constitute a challenge to the 'expert' perspectives of professionals.

Challenging 'expert' perspectives

We have seen that a change in perspective can have an important impact on how services are designed. If needs are defined in practitioners' terms, for example, then disabled people may find that they are provided with 'care'. If need is defined by disabled people themselves, the requirement may be understood rather differently – as 'personal assistance' to enable independent living. Morris (1995) has argued in the Reader Chapter 19 that an agenda of 'care' can construct disabled people as dependent, passive and a burden. She introduces the concept of 'independent living' to stress the continued ability to make choices and fulfil a wider range of roles. Disabled people who are seeking independent living are active and self-determined. This means, for example, that a person who is restricted by impairment from tying their shoelaces is not dismissed as 'dependent'. Simply because you can't tie your shoelaces, it doesn't mean you can't have a say about what shoes to wear or when to put them on. Independent living choices include having a say in who is to assist, when assistance is needed and how this assistance is required. The language has changed from 'care' to 'assistance', as the emphasis has changed from dependence to independence. The disabled person becomes the 'expert' on their own situation.

In Unit 10 Ken Simons is quoted as saying that advocates should be unconditional allies of the person they are supporting. People acting in other capacities may not be able to take this on. Lawyers, for instance, are only prepared to advocate for clients when some conditions are met. For example, most lawyers will not tell lies for clients and most will draw the line at supporting a client through a course of action they think has no chance of a successful outcome.

The term 'self-advocacy' suggests that people advocate for themselves in ways that allow them to put forward their own views as they themselves see them. Perhaps this is so, but many so-called 'self-advocacy' groups rely heavily on the advice and support of paid or volunteer workers. Inevitably, this advice influences the way self-advocating people speak for themselves. Sometimes this may mean that they self-advocate for what seems possible, rather than for what they would prefer. This is not a strategy especially associated with self-advocacy in health and social care. Life often confronts people with situations where they can choose between demanding exactly what they want and getting nothing, and demanding rather less than they want and getting something. What you get often depends on what other people will agree to. Deciding how far to compromise in order to be successful in the planning system is something that taxes many self-advocacy groups. The dilemma is nicely captured in the title of an article by Edna Conlan called 'Shaking hands with the devil' (1996).

All this is to say that it is very difficult to draw a line between advocacy and the kinds of self-advocacy that involve support workers or facilitators. However, two sets of ideas that are associated with self-advocacy rather than with advocacy are that practising self-advocacy helps people to develop their confidence and their self-esteem, and that self-advocacy is a process through which the people concerned learn valuable skills (The Open University, 1990b, p. 101).

In the words of Suzy Croft and Peter Beresford, who have been important figures in the English self-advocacy movement:

> *Developing our own accounts ... is the starting point for our empowerment. It means putting together our views, our versions of things. We begin by articulating our wants and experiences. Once we put our individual accounts together, we become aware of the similarities and overlaps with other people's. We discover there's nothing strange or special about us. It isn't just me. I'm not the only woman who feels lonely stuck at home with a young baby. Other people have the same problems living on income support. Our thoughts and ideas aren't just moans, grumbles and gossip. They aren't merely anecdotal or apocryphal. They don't have to be hidden, secret and illegitimate. They are helpful and important. We have the right to express them. We begin to see that they have validity alongside other more powerful accounts. We have our side of the story to tell too.*

> *(Croft and Beresford, 1993, p. 131)*

Croft and Beresford are commenting on the development of self-confidence and self-esteem through self-advocacy. The other important aspect is the learning of skills.

Some of the skills you could develop through self-advocacy include:

- **Social relationship skills** – how to get on with each other, how to make relationships with people you are negotiating with and so on, how to relate to each other in decision-making meetings.

- **Communication skills** – how to prepare and give a presentation, for example.

- **Organisational skills** – how to conduct meetings, write minutes, do forward planning, and so on.

4.2 A self-advocacy group

In Activity 4 you will be asked to listen to an audio cassette about the development of a self-advocacy group of people with learning disabilities. The cassette you will hear features the self-advocacy group at Leavesden Hospital in Hertfordshire. This was a large 'mental handicap' hospital like Lennox Castle (Unit 16).

A meeting of the Leavesden self-advocacy group

The formation of the group more or less coincided with plans to close the hospital and disperse its 'inmates' into the community. Thinking about how former inmates were going to accommodate themselves to life outside may have encouraged staff and management to take the idea of self-advocacy seriously. The cassette was made in 1990, three or four years after the self-advocacy group was established, and at a time when self-advocacy groups were still rather controversial. The members of the Leavesden group now live in the community but many are still members of self-advocacy groups linked into the national People First network. You saw some work that has come from this organisation in Section 1 on designing picture-supported information.

Activity 4   **Self-advocacy at Leavesden**

Allow about 25 minutes

Find Audio Cassette 6, side 2, which is about the Leavesden self-advocacy group. Two members of the group, Ronnie Palmer and Ronnie Lewis, and the group's facilitator (Dave Lewis) tell you about the development of the group, and what it did in the way of organising events and influencing services. For this activity pay particular attention to what the cassette tells you about the way the self-advocacy group provided opportunities for its members to develop and display their skills and confidence. Jot down your own notes about this as you listen to the recording.

Comment   Here is what Fiona Williams said about the recording in another OU course:

> *People gain a lot from their membership of the group, as two of the tape contributors indicate: 'it's made my life completely good really'. 'I get out more things about how I feel'. Other attractions of the group at a personal level include opportunities to:*
>
> * *attend a self-advocacy conference*
>
> * *take part in leisure and sports activities such as drama, football, hockey and running*
>
> * *enjoy parties and pub lunches*
>
> * *get help with personal problems*
>
> * *develop more two-way relationships and friendships with staff.*
>
> *(The Open University, 1990a, p. 20)*

The late Anita Binns, a leading member of the self-advocacy movement among people with learning difficulties

The recording gave you a glimpse of the way the Leavesden group facilitated self-development, at least with regard to the two leading members of the group who spoke on the tape. Think back to the discussion on providing information to help people access services in Section 1. Self-advocacy gives people the confidence and the support to take advantage of services in a way that simply providing information does not. The next activity is designed to give you a better picture of the importance of self-advocacy in terms of someone's biography. It features Anita Binns, another graduate of the self-advocacy movement, but this time in Nottingham and later Gateshead.

Activity 5   **Anita's story**

Allow about 15 minutes   Find Offprint 28 'Anita's story', which is derived from an interview with the late Anita Binns. When you read it you will see that the story falls into a 'before' and 'after' pattern. As you read it, try jotting down what Anita could do after she developed the skills of self-advocacy, which she didn't seem able to do before. The reference to 'Skills' in the offprint is a reference to the 'Skills for self-advocacy programme': a training programme for self-advocacy.

Comment   Here are some of the befores and afters you might have noted:

Before	After
Couldn't stand up for herself without having a blazing row	Could firmly and calmly put a social worker in his place
Allowed herself to be stigmatised and put upon, treated as an inferior and given the least desirable tasks to do	Wouldn't allow this to happen again
Didn't know how to advocate for herself	Knows very well how to advocate for herself
Couldn't have helped others to self-advocate	Regularly helps others develop these skills

Didn't have any idea of her rights, or of the responsibilities which might go with these	Can assert her rights and can address a conference on this topic
Couldn't have addressed a conference	Is a seasoned conference performer
(Probably) couldn't have told her life story in such a lucid way	Is able to tell her life story as a story of personal success, and as the success of a movement
Didn't have a very interesting life story to tell	Now has a very interesting life story to tell and lots of opportunities to tell it – at conferences, in the publications of People First and The Open University, and in other publications

A quicker way of saying all this would be to say that through self-advocacy Anita has transformed herself into a person likely to engage the interests of others and able to make a valuable contribution to *their* lives.

Key points

- The movement for self-advocacy was one of the most important developments in health and social care in the 1980s and 1990s.

- Self-advocacy means speaking for yourself, rather than having someone speak on your behalf. It usually implies doing so with the support of a self-advocacy group.

- It is often difficult to distinguish self-advocacy from advocacy when support workers or facilitators are employed to assist self-advocacy groups.

- Two things claimed for self-advocacy but not for advocacy are that practising self-advocacy helps people gain confidence and self-esteem, and develop valuable skills.

This section has been about self-advocacy groups and self-advocacy skills. It ended by considering the importance of these for self-development.

Study skills: Ways of reporting (Part 1)

Whether as a carer, or as a student of care, you need to become skilled both at reading and writing reports of care situations. A report is never simply 'the facts' of the situation. Any report has to select from many potentially relevant facts. Moreover, the way the report is written (or spoken) inevitably gives a particular 'slant' to the story. It makes a lot of difference *who* is reporting *to whom*, and *what* they are trying to report about and *why*.

You can easily see this by looking back at Anita Binns's story. Take just the first four paragraphs of Offprint 28; they outline an incident involving Anita at an Adult Training Centre (ATC). This is an oral report of the incident by Anita herself, recorded on audio tape in an interview.

Activity 6   **Ways of reporting**

Allow about 30 minutes

Read the first four paragraphs of Offprint 28 again and make notes of what you think happened. Then write a few lines presenting a 'report' of the incident.

After that read the five reports below.

1   It was decided that the most appropriate option for Ms Binns was sheltered accommodation with opportunities for employment. However, with arrangements already well advanced she refused point blank to consider them. After an emotional outburst she severed her links with the Centre.

2   The meeting was badly handled. The client had not been prepared in advance for a relocation. Despite best efforts to provide emotional support, management's unsympathetic, heavy-handed approach led to a complete breakdown of relations.

3   Anita Binns is a challenging client, prone to sharp, unpredictable mood swings. She is suspicious of strange people and situations and finds it difficult to cope with change. She is resistant to efforts to help her and quickly becomes confrontational.

4   Although she lacks self-confidence and is easily overcome by her feelings, Anita is a shrewd judge of people and situations. She quickly recognised that Centre management, for their own convenience, intended to dispatch her to alternative provision without due consultation or respect for her wishes and rights. She put up a stout resistance and was not cowed by threats of suspension.

5   A. Binns. Difficult client. Refused appropriate provision. Became confrontational. Temporary suspension from the Centre.

These reports were made up using only the information in Anita's account. Is your report at all like any of these? If not, why do you think yours is different? Does it have a different slant? If so, what is your slant?

Look back at these five reports and at your own. For each try to answer these questions.

*   *Who* would write a report of this kind?
*   *To whom* would it be written?
*   *What* is it a report about?
*   *Why* would a report of this kind be written? What is its purpose?

Comment   These made-up reports were written to show how differently the same events could be reported.

1   This kind of report might perhaps be written by a worker at the ATC, as case notes on Anita which might be read by other agencies. The report focuses on the efforts made by the ATC to meet Anita's needs and her unco-operative response. Its purpose is to demonstrate that the ATC did a reasonable job of discharging its duties towards Anita.

2   This type of report would certainly not be written by the ATC management. More likely, it would be written by Anita's social worker, to be read by social work colleagues. The report is about the failure of the ATC management to handle communications with Anita sensitively. Although in her own account Anita suggests that it was the social worker who should have told her about the move, there is no mention of this, only of the emotional support the social worker offered. The purpose seems to be to criticise the regime at the ATC.

3   This kind of report might perhaps be written by someone at the ATC with responsibility for assessing Anita, to be read by colleagues who have dealings with her. Its focus is on Anita herself rather than the incident. It reads motives and personal characteristics into her actions and slots her into psychological categories. The message is that Anita's problems lie within herself, rather than in difficult circumstances or the way she has been treated.

4   This is a more sympathetic account by someone with responsibility for assessing Anita. Perhaps it is to be read by colleagues at a case conference. Instead of focusing on inner weaknesses, it is about her strengths. It criticises ATC management and commends Anita's resourcefulness and resilience.

5   This might be a routine record made by a member of ATC staff, to be read only if queries about Anita's case should arise later. Like the first report it emphasises that the ATC discharged its duties properly and that the problems arose from Anita's side.

Notice that just changing small things, for example, how Anita is referred to, alters the way the reports read. She is referred to variously as Ms Binns, the client, Anita Binns, Anita, A. Binns. Each style positions the report writer differently in relation to Anita. Were you able to work out who you were reporting as and to whom, and what the purpose of your report was?

The other account to mention is Anita's own. She is reporting as one person in conversation with another, trying to draw on the listener's sympathy. Her account emphasises the people involved in the situation and their relationship to her. She focuses on the unfairness and insensitivity of others and her own emotional reactions, but also her resilience. It is actually quite hard to get to grips with what happened at the ATC. Anita has not provided some of the basics that a report requires. She does not establish the general context and the specific circumstances. Nor is it very clear where her account is leading, or what its purpose is. This is understandable, since she has difficulties expressing herself and wasn't setting out to give a 'report' anyway. But you get a useful insight into why a report needs to indicate context and purpose. Although the other reports above do not spell out context and purpose explicitly, they signal them in subtle ways, as you have seen.

Study skills: Ways of reporting (Part 2)

Clearly, the same incident can give rise to very different accounts. It makes a lot of difference who is reporting to whom and why. As a reader, you need to develop a sensitivity to what lies behind the reports you read. The words on the page are only part of the story. Becoming a skilled reader means being able to read 'critically', weighing up the quality of the case that is being made at the same time as taking in its details.

Conclusion

This unit started by posing four main questions; the first of these asked:

- **Who needs information about services? Where can information be found?**

In Section 1, we looked at the very varied information needs that people may have, and how these relate to the different roles that they occupy. Care workers need information in order to function in their various professional capacities, and all of us need information to enable us to cope with a variety of personal and social situations. Using characters associated with the Grove Health Centre, we looked at the complex webs of information that they each needed and had to find their way around.

The next question, arising from this discussion, was:

- **Why can it be difficult to find out about services? And what measures can be taken to improve the quality and dissemination of information about services?**

In Section 2 we saw that it is difficult to know where to look for information. But when information *is* provided about care services, it often fails to reach its intended audience, or if it does it may not be paid attention to, or not be understood. Sharing information effectively needs thought, to ensure that written and other material is delivered through the right channels and is properly accessible to the people it is designed to reach. Measures can be taken to improve the quality and dissemination of information about services, and different communication needs can be met – but only if providers of information recognise and respond to the diversity of their potential audience.

The third broad question addressed the issue of planning:

- **How can service users be more fully involved in the planning, management and evaluation of the services they use?**

Section 3 considered how service users could be involved in the complex and demanding tasks of service planning in their localities. It is important that service users have a voice in the planning process, so that their knowledge and experience can play a part in the planning process. Otherwise we are likely to end up with services that people do not want, or cannot use.

Lastly, the fourth question asked:

- **What skills and what support do service users need in order to be more fully involved?**

In Section 4 we explored one way of supporting service user involvement through the development of self-advocacy groups. Here service users can, with support, develop a range of skills which not only help them to advocate effectively for those they represent, but increase personal self-confidence and self-esteem. Self-advocacy acknowledges the experience that service users have, allowing them to speak for themselves on matters of concern to them, and giving them an active role in the system.

Study skills: The summer break

Just to remind you, there is a six-week gap between TMA 05 and TMA 06. That means you can spread the four units of Block 6 over six weeks. This is to give you some space to take a summer break if you want to. But obviously you don't want to lose momentum too much. You will need to keep an eye on your progress through the block. Anyway, we hope you will feel refreshed after this brief slackening of the pace.

References

Althuser (1971) *Lenin and Philosophy and other essays*, London, New Left Books.

Beresford, P. and Campbell, P. (1990) 'Disabled people, service users, user involvement and representation', *Disability and Society*, Vol. 9, No. 3, pp. 315–25.

Bowling, A. (1993) *What People Say About Prioritising Health Services*, King's Fund, London.

Brighton Polytechnic (1992) *The Evaluation of the Whitehawk Project*, report presented to the Brighton Health Authority and TEED, Brighton Polytechnic, Brighton.

Brindle, D. (1995) 'The consultation cure', *Guardian*, 10 May, p. 10.

Bromley Health (1995) *Local NHS Care Purchasing and Prioritising from the Perspective of Bromley Residents*, Bromley Health, Hayes.

Campbell, P. (1996) 'The history of the user movement in the United Kingdom' in Heller, T., Reynolds, J., Gomm, R., Muston, R. and Pattison, S. (eds) *Mental Health Matters: A Reader*, Macmillan, Basingstoke.

Crawley, B. (1988) *The Growing Voice: A Survey of Self-Advocacy Groups in ATCs and Hospitals: Great Britain*, CMH Publications, London.

Conlan, E. (1996) 'Shaking hands with the devil' in Read, J. and Reynolds, J. (eds) *Speaking Our Minds: An Anthology*, Macmillan, Basingstoke.

Croft, S. and Beresford, P. (1993) *Getting Involved: A Practical Manual*, Joseph Rowntree Foundation, York.

Cutts, M. and Maher, C. (1980) *Writing Plain English*, Plain English Campaign, London.

Gottlieb, B. (ed.) (1981) *Social Networks and Social Support*, Sage, London.

Jones, A., Jeyasingham, D. and Rajasooriya, S. (2002) *Invisible families: The strengths and needs of Black families in which young people have caring responsibilities*, The Policy Press.

Lazarsfeld, P., Berelson, B. and Gaudet, H. (1944) *The People's Choice*, Columbia University Press, New York.

Lindsey, M. and Russell, O. (1999) *Once a day one or more people with learning disabilities are likely to be in contact with your primary healthcare team. How can you help them?*, Department of Health, London.

MacIntosh, M. (1987) 'Effective media for voluntary sector promotion', *Communicate!*, No. 27, pp. 5–6.

Moffatt, V. (1993) *Keep It Simple: A Guide to Creating Accessible Documents for People with Learning Difficulties*, Southwark Information, London Borough of Southwark.

Ogden, J. (1996) 'Open court', *Health Services Journal*, 9 May, p. 12.

People First (1994) *Making Information and Words Easier to Understand*, People First, London.

RNIB, priorities in health and social care for blind and partially sighted people, http://www.rnib.org.uk/campaign/welcome.htm [accessed:24.6.02] http://www.rnib.org.uk/campaign/improvlives/report.htm [accessed: 24.6.02]

Robson, G. (1987) 'Nagging: models of advocacy' in Barker, I. and Peck, E. (eds) *Power in Strange Places: User Empowerment in Mental Health Services*, Good Practices in Mental Health, London.

The Open University (1990a) K668 *Mental Handicap: Changing Perspectives*, Media Notes, The Open University, Milton Keynes.

The Open University (1990b) K668 *Mental Handicap: Changing Perspectives*, Workbook 3, *Transitions and Change*, The Open University, Milton Keynes.

University of Warwick (1993) *Caring is Jargon Free*, Social Care Centre for Practice and Staff Development, University of Warwick, Coventry.

Whitehead, M. (1989) *Swimming Upstream: Trends and Prospects in Education for Health*, Research Report No. 5, King's Fund, London.

Wiltshire Social Services (1993) *The Friendly Guide to Care in the Community for People with Learning Difficulties*, Wiltshire Social Services, Salisbury.

Acknowledgements

Grateful acknowledgement is made to the following sources for permission to reproduce material in this unit:

Illustrations

p. 19: Courtesy of the Partially Sighted Society; *p. 22*: *Oi! It's My Assessment*, People First; *p. 36*: Estate of the late Anita Binns.

Unit 23

Confidentiality: Managing Personal Information

Originally prepared for the course team by Roger Gomm

Revised by Danielle Turney and Marion Reichart

While you are working on Unit 23, you will need:
- Offprints Book
- Wallchart

Contents

Introduction

In Unit 22, we spent some time thinking about how information about service provision is collected and why it can be difficult for both service users and service planners/providers to get hold of the information they need. Here, we continue with the theme of information but look at it from a slightly different angle. Our concern in this unit is with the way personal information about each of us, as users of health and social care services, is collected, stored and – on occasions – shared. We begin by thinking about why such information is needed and how it is used. But as soon as we start to consider these questions, another issue immediately presents itself – confidentiality. What happens to information once it is 'on record'? How can health and social care agencies work effectively, but also 'safely' with this information about us? How can we know that information that we have given is going to be treated with respect and that confidentiality will be preserved? Confidentiality is one of the values stressed by all professional bodies concerned with health and social care, and in all the major syllabuses for training health and social care practitioners. Its importance was highlighted in Unit 21, where breaches of confidentiality by Ruth were a key issue. And it will also be a key theme in this unit where we look at one agency's confidentiality policy and at some of the complexities that arise when confidentiality may need to be broken.

This unit, then, is about personal information and its management. We may accept the need for health and social care professionals to ask us personal questions, but this information is generally not just stored in their heads: they write things down and create records. One reason why recording is an important topic is that so much effort in health and social care goes into record making and record keeping. The average district general hospital holds about 200,000 sets of case notes. Between 10,000 and 20,000 of these will be in use in any one month.

The average district general hospital holds about 200,000 sets of case notes

About 15 per cent of health care costs arise from handling records (Audit Commission, 1995a): about £10 million per NHS trust per year (Benson, 1997). However, this does not take into account the fact that doctors and nurses spend just over one quarter of their working time composing and scrutinising records (Audit Commission, 1995b). Moreover, social workers who mainly assess clients' and carers' needs probably spend a larger percentage of their time doing this (Department of Health, 1994a). And people who work in the Benefits Agency do little else but make and consult records.

By contrast, some people who work in health and social care, such as care assistants in some residential homes, spend very little time reading records and make very few records themselves. Nonetheless, there will be records concerning them and their activities. For care assistants, for example, the kinds of records made in a residential home will define their jobs and will be evidence about what they have done. And in some residential homes, such as Liberty of Earley House (see Unit 8), care assistants are quite heavily involved in record making. The category of people in health and social care who do the least in the way of recording are those who receive the services. But records about them are central to the workings of health and social care organisations.

Section 1 of this unit looks at the different functions records perform in health and social care. By showing what is done through making records it answers the question of why records are important. This section also looks at who has access to an individual's records, and the role that service users can play in the making and management of their own records. Lastly, we consider what makes records useful to the people they concern.

Section 2 extends the discussion about who should have access to records by considering confidentiality of information. This discussion is continued in Section 3 where we look at an example of a confidentiality policy and consider some of the practical and ethical issues that arise when you try and implement such a policy. Section 4 examines the limits of confidentiality, when the health and safety of some people require the disclosure of private information about others.

The Conclusion rounds off the unit by reviewing the way in which the core questions have been addressed. However, the unit does not exhaust all that will be said about either recording or confidentiality in this block. As you will see, one of the most important functions of recording is to make people accountable for their actions. Accountability is the topic of Unit 24. Confidentiality features again in Unit 25, the skills unit for this block.

Core questions

- Why do we need records and what functions do records and recording perform in health and social care organisations?

- What do the users of services need from records and how can recording best serve their needs?

- Who controls information and the way it is shared?

- What is a duty of confidentiality and how does a confidentiality policy work?

- How can a balance be struck between respecting the privacy of one individual by keeping recorded information confidential, and protecting the interests of others who may have a legitimate need to know this information?

Section 1

Why do we need records? The functions of recording in health and social care

This section looks at the different functions that records perform in health and social care. We are probably all familiar with the idea that records are kept about us for different purposes but have you stopped to think about the many different contexts in which information about you may be collected?

Activity 1 **On the record**

Allow about 10 minutes Spend a few minutes thinking about the different situations where records may be kept about you. Who holds records about you? How much and what kind of information would you expect there to be in those records?

Comment We will all come up with different lists, but you may have included some of the types of records that follow. If you are registered with a GP then he or she will have a set of medical notes about you. These will probably include any hospital test results, referral letters etc. You may also have records at your local hospital, covering in- and out-patient treatment over the years. In addition, there may be financial records at a bank, building society or credit company. If you are in employment, there will be a personnel file at work; alternatively, if you have been receiving benefits, details about your circumstances will be held by the relevant agency. Car owners' details are held by DVLA. You may have insurance policies which will mean more records ... In addition, of course, as OU students, there will be records containing a variety of information about you: the courses you have registered for, your progression through those courses (by now, TMA PT3 forms which record your tutor's comments on written assignments will have become a regular part of your lives!), and so on.

So for most of us, there will be a number of contexts in which we are the subject of records. And if we are also clients of health and social care services, the range of records that may be kept extends still further. But what kinds of records are we referring to – and why are so many different sorts of records required anyway? To start answering this question, we need to think about the functions that records of different sorts can perform. As we will see, the kinds of records that are kept will be dependent on the functions that they are intended to fulfil. So in the first section, we will look at one very important form of record – the care plan – and use that to start thinking about the different functions that record keeping can perform.

1.1 A care plan as a record

You will come across many different ways to record information within health and social care. One common type of record is the 'care plan'. You saw an example of a care plan in Unit 3 which set out the services that would be provided for Alice by her home carer, Mary, and you will be looking at another example, the care plan for Arthur Durrant, in the next activity. For the purposes of this activity, we are not going to think about the appropriateness or otherwise of the care outlined in the plan, but will be considering how Arthur's care plan works as a record. We can then use it to identify some of the different functions that records can perform. When it comes to deciding the adequacy of a care plan *as a record,* you first need to ask questions about what, exactly, this care plan is trying to do. Then you can decide how well it does it.

Activity 2   A care plan for Arthur Durrant

Allow about 10 minutes

Offprint 29 shows the kind of care plan which might have been written for Arthur Durrant shortly after his discharge from hospital, by Dev Sharma, the social worker who acts as care (or case) manager for him. You met Arthur Durrant and his daughter Lynne in Block 1 of this course. For this activity read through the care plan and make some notes about what you think its purposes are. You might start by considering who the plan seems to be written for.

Comment

At first sight, at least, the plan seems to be written for Arthur to read. The term 'you' meaning 'Arthur' is used. It tells Arthur what services it has been agreed will be provided. In that sense the care plan is a set of promises to Arthur: a kind of contract such that if these promises are broken he will have grounds to complain. (Note that the plan says that Arthur has been given a copy of the departmental complaints procedures.) Where records make promises, they make certain people accountable for keeping those promises. *Making people accountable* is often an important function of records.

The plan also describes some actions which have been taken by Dev Sharma: for example, that he has arranged for an occupational therapist to visit, and that he has checked Arthur's welfare benefits situation. These are actions a good social worker should have taken, so in this way the plan shows that Dev has done what he should have done. If his manager looked at the plan this would be apparent. So the plan not only makes Dev and the social services department accountable to Arthur, but also makes Dev *accountable* to his employers.

In the plan Dev Sharma makes promises on behalf of the social services department. In that sense he *authorises* social services expenditure. As a care manager he may have a budget to spend (Downey, 1995) or he may have had to apply to his senior for permission to spend money on buying in home care services. Either way, this care plan *authorises* social services expenditure. Arthur's signature at the end also gives authorisation. It says, 'I agree to this package of care'.

In fact, a great deal on the form is outside Dev Sharma's authority. He has no power to commit the housing department, the community nursing services, the consultant in charge of diabetes, hospital transport or the wheelchair technicians. The last four belong to the health service, not to social services. So those entries on the plan merely report what other people have agreed to do. The official guidance for social care assessment (Department of Health, 1991a; Northern Ireland Office, 1991) makes social workers responsible not only for assessing their clients' needs for social care but for other services as well. Look at the bottom of the form. There is a circulation list, which includes other practitioners and other agencies. Circulating this plan to these others ensures that it performs a function of *co-ordination*. It tells everyone involved what has been agreed with Arthur – which is something they all need to know.

A large number of care plans like this would also be useful for *monitoring* what was happening in the disability care team of which Dev Sharma is a member. Records are often used as the basis for monitoring how an agency is performing. So, although the plan looks as if it was written just for Arthur to read, it also assumes other readers, particularly where it has a function of accountability, authorisation, co-ordination and monitoring.

So far, we have identified four key functions of record making, based on our consideration of Arthur's care plan. But this does not exhaust the range of functions that records can perform. Indeed, in some ways this care plan misses out one of the commonest uses for recording: *collating and storing information for decision making*. By the time this care plan was written, most of the information that was needed to inform plans for Arthur's care had already been collected – probably through a 'community care assessment' co-ordinated by Dev Sharma. Dev would then be able to use this information in drawing up a specific care plan. Medical records are perhaps the best example of records that collate and store information for decision making, particularly where they record the results of examinations and diagnostic tests.

Moving away from the care plan, to consider records more generally, we can identify three more functions. Records can be used as a means of making practice more systematic, to promote reflection, personal growth and/or professional development, and as a means of making relationships. A record rarely performs only one of these functions and in practice the same record may perform many of them all at the same time. Table 1 draws on a range of examples, including some from the Grove Health Centre you visited in Unit 22, to illustrate these different functions.

Table 1   Some functions of record making

Functions	Examples
1. Accountability *Records may say who is responsible for doing what, and what they have (or haven't) done.*	• In order to provide adequate respite care for Mr Li, the residential home Eventide is required to do certain things and keep records saying whether these things have been done. • When Michelle McDonald signed on for welfare benefits, there was a section at the end of the claim form where she was asked to sign that the details filled in on the form were accurate. She is then accountable for the honesty of the claim and there are fines and prison sentences for false claims.

2. Authorisation
    Records may indicate who has a right, and perhaps a duty, to do what with regard to whom.

- Pat Walsh broke her wrist in a car accident. As this was a bad break it needed setting under anaesthetic, so she was asked to sign a consent form to authorise health personnel to carry out the operation.

- Other examples include references and education certificates used in gaining employment; assessment forms which record the eligibility of someone to receive a benefit or service; a 'letter of administration' or 'power of attorney', which allows a person to manage someone else's financial affairs when they are unable to do so.

3. Decision making about service users
    Records may assemble and store the information on which decisions about clients should be based and information about decisions which have been made.

- Records fulfilling this function would include the records of any diagnostic tests – such as the x-ray of Pat Walsh's broken wrist – and other medical records which would be used as the basis for decisions about treatment.

- In addition virtually all records about clients of social services, like Arthur Durrant or Thomas Li, such as assessment forms, fulfil this function.

4. Monitoring the performance of services
    Records may assemble and store information about how and how well an organisation is performing.

- The kinds of records which show how many people visit an agency; what kinds of people receive what kind of treatment; what the gender and ethnic mix of the client group is; the case loads of the workers; how many violent incidents happen each year; how many clients achieve satisfactory outcomes.

5. Co-ordinating activities
    Records may indicate who should be doing what and when so that people can gear their activities one with another.

- Arthur's care plan which involves care delivered by more than one person or agency is a good example.

- Other examples include referral forms and letters from one agency to another, for example, from a GP to a specialist.

6. Systematic practice
    Record making makes practice systematic.

    • The kind of form that Dev Sharma completes when assessing the financial situation of a client tells him what questions to ask. In this sense it structures his perception of what is relevant, and organises what he does. Forms and checklists like this are common in record-making systems in health and care work.

7. Reflection, personal growth and/or professional development, and as means of making relationships
    Making a record makes sense of an experience or a situation. In making a record two people get to know each other.

    • You may keep a diary in which you record your thoughts and feelings about events in your personal and/or professional life. You can use such a diary as the basis for reflecting on your practice and promoting personal and professional development.

    • Life history books (Unit 14) are an obvious example of a record designed to help make sense of an experience. Looking together at a life history book can also be a successful way to develop a relationship between service user and worker.

1.2 Different purposes, different records: how paperwork expands

What is a 'good' record, and what makes an effective record system? How much time and money should be spent on record making and keeping? Useful questions, but difficult to answer without first deciding what particular records are for.

As we noted in the last section, records are made for different purposes, so good practice depends on what the purpose of making the record is. Adequate records for pinning down accountability are not necessarily good records for making decisions about care. And good records for reminiscence work are certainly not good records for establishing whether someone is eligible for a particular service and hence can be authorised to receive it. Imagine trying to operate a welfare benefits system where applications were made through presenting life history books. A recording system adequately fulfilling all the functions listed in Table 1 to the same degree would be much too expensive to operate. Perhaps a good general question to ask about any kind of record is, 'Does it record what the readers of the records need to know in terms of the purpose the record is supposed to fulfil, *and no more than this*?'

The 'no more than this' is important in two ways: one relating to expense, and the other to privacy and confidentiality. We look at confidentiality later in the unit so here we will concentrate on the point that making and looking after records is extremely expensive and very time-consuming. Community care assessments under the terms of the NHS and Community Care Act 1990 can sometimes take five hours or more to complete. As social services and social work departments also now assess carers under the Carers (Recognition and Services) Act 1995, they will be spending even more time in making records (Watson and Taylor, 1996).

In health and social care there is a built-in demand for more and more record making. One way of understanding this is to reconsider what is listed in Table 1. Whatever the problem is, there is a tendency to seek a solution by recording more information. An example may help show how this happens: Mr Li has been assessed under the NHS and Community Care Act 1990 and found to be in need of various services. A care plan has been drawn up to specify what will be provided by the local authority and other services. One of the services Mr Li has been offered is respite care at the Eventide residential home. But he is thinking of turning this down, as he does not know if there will be anyone there he can talk to in Cantonese or who can prepare the food he likes. Dev Sharma would like to reassure Mr Li that the service is used by a range of people from different ethnic backgrounds and that his dietary needs can be met, and has data from the county's ethnic monitoring surveys to support this. Having read their latest inspection report, he is confident that Eventide offers a good standard of care – better than one of the other homes in the area, which had recently received a poor report. In addition to respite care, Mr Li has been assessed for home care and referral to a day centre has also been discussed. Mr Li is also going to need some OT support. Providing this range of services will require a degree of co-ordination by Dev as care manager.

How might this situation lead to increased paperwork? We noted earlier in the unit that records perform a number of functions (these were summarised in Table 1). At each stage in the scenario, we can see how there are different demands for information – and at each stage, that information will need to be recorded. The following list identifies some of the records associated with work with just one service user. So now imagine the paperwork associated with all the clients in one team, one agency, one county … Suddenly, that's an awful lot of paper!

- Within social and health services, managers want to ensure that practitioners and agencies are fully accountable to those they serve. To achieve this, they may require practitioners like Dev to keep more – and more detailed - records which clearly set out what they have promised, and which also record what they have done. So Dev will complete a care plan for Mr Li, and in addition he will routinely record when he has contact with him, any decisions made and action taken, keep copies of any correspondence, etc.

- To promote anti-discriminatory practice, agencies need to know which services are used by different groups in the community - for example, whether services are used by people from different minority ethnic groups – and to find this out, they will need monitoring systems. Completion of ethnic monitoring forms may therefore become a routine procedure with each new referral to the service. So it is likely that each service that Dev has identified in Mr Li's care plan will want ethnic monitoring information for their own records. Service managers can then use this information to assess whether and how well the service is reaching the different community groups. And, as we noted above, Dev can also use this information to reassure Mr Li that Eventide can offer him appropriate care.

- Dev also referred to inspection reports about Eventide and another local home. Concern about standards in residential care usually leads to suggestions that inspections should be more rigorous (Unit

8). More rigorous inspection would mean more records made by the residential establishments for inspection teams to look at, and more records made by the inspection teams themselves.

- Mr Li's care package makes use of both health and social care services. As noted in Unit 22, it is important for health and social care services to be properly *co-ordinated*. So there is a demand that they plan together and record their deliberations and conclusions.

- Then, from a rather different direction, there is a demand that service users should be treated as the unique individuals they are, and that for this purpose records should be produced through biographical or autobiographical approaches (Unit 16 and function 7 on Table 1). Such approaches have the potential to generate very weighty records indeed and can be a long time in the making. Dev, however, was able to ask Dr Li to collaborate with her father in writing a short account of his life, which Dev found very helpful in understanding Mr Li's beliefs and preferences.

- Everybody wants *decisions* about health and social care to be based on the best possible evidence, so there is always a demand that practitioners collect more evidence for decision making. This is particularly marked in the health service, where 'evidence-based medicine' is regarded as a way of improving the quality of care and the efficiency of resource use (National Health Service Executive, 1996b; Walshe and Ham, 1997). However, evidence-based practice is becoming increasingly important in other branches of social care. What evidence-based practice means is that treatments or other interventions are chosen on the basis of evidence that they work. That means collecting evidence to see what does work, and looking at each case for evidence that a particular intervention is likely to work – and of course, recording all this.

- Governments always hope to improve the performance of health and social services by improving their management. But to manage, managers need information so that they can *monitor* what is happening and to inform the planning process.

Yet in the face of all these demands for *more* records there is a demand that health and social care services spend *less* time on paperwork and *more* time on direct care. This demand often comes from the same people who are, in effect, asking for more recording to be done. Taken one at a time, each case suggested above for making more detailed records is quite convincing. But proceeding on all these fronts at the same time very quickly leads to two practical problems. First, if health and social care practitioners spend more time recording, they cannot spend as much time doing other things. Second, the more there is recorded, the longer the records take to consult, and the less likely it is that people will find the time to use the information which has been recorded.

However, it is difficult to decide what is 'the minimum necessary' to record, because different groups make different demands on records systems. Governments, managers (of different kinds), auditors, practitioners, workplace trainers, researchers, regulatory bodies, equal opportunities committees, organised groups of service users, individual service users and informal carers may all want different matters recorded and more of this and less of that.

Key points

- Records can fulfil a number of different functions in health and social care.

- Sometimes the process of collecting the information to make the record may be more important than the record itself.

- Records made for different purposes require different processes and formats for recording.

- Most records fulfil several functions at one and the same time, but a recording system which is ideal for one purpose may not be ideal for another.

- Since recording is costly, deciding what is the minimum necessary is an important matter, but since there are competing demands about what should be recorded, the minimum necessary is usually quite a lot.

1.3 Making use of records: what service users and carers might want from records

So far, we have looked at records mainly from the viewpoint of those who provide and manage care. This section looks at the way recorded information might be useful to service users and informal carers.

A service user may simply want to know what has been said about them or to check what has been agreed (for example, in relation to service provision). Written care plans and formal records can help here – but to be useful, they need to be both **accessible** and **understandable** to the person to whom they apply.

Access to records

Let us assume that Wayne is concerned about the information that is held by his GP, Dr Li, about his drug use. There is now a range of legislation setting out what rights he has in relation to information about himself. The most recent provisions are the Data Protection Act 1998 and the Freedom of Information Act 2000 which together give individuals the right to access a wide range of information held on them by public bodies (whether this information is stored electronically or on paper). In relation to information held by health authorities, there are exceptions to rights of access, of which the following are the most important.

Data Protection Act 1998: Protection and Use of Patient Information

Part 3 Rights of Access to Personal Data

(iii)   where disclosing the personal data would reveal information which relates to and identifies another person (for example that a relative had provided certain information) unless that person has consented to the disclosure or it is reasonable to comply with the request without that consent. The factors listed in section 7(6) should be considered in determining whether it would be reasonable in all the circumstances. These provisions do not apply where the person to be identified is a health professional who has either compiled or contributed to either the record or the care of the patient; in the case of personal data consisting of information about the physical or mental health or condition of the data subject (i.e. most information held by NHS bodies) the Data Protection (Subject Access Modification) (Health) Order 2000 provides exemptions from the subject access rights in two situations:

(a) where permitting access to the data would be likely to cause serious harm to the physical or mental health or condition of the data subject or any other person (which may include a health professional);

(b) where the request for access is made by another on behalf of the data subject, such as a parent for a child, access can be refused if the data subject had either provided the information in the expectation it would not be disclosed to the applicant or had indicated it should not be so disclosed, or if the data was obtained as a result of any examination or investigation to which the data subject consented on the basis that information would not be so disclosed.

 Information accessed from Department of Health website (06.06.02) http://www.doh.gov.UK/dpa98/

 Effectively this means that doctors may refuse the patient access to all or part of the records if it is their medical opinion that access may cause serious physical or mental harm to the patient or someone else. And access may be denied if this would disclose information about a third party without his or her consent. For example, on one occasion Wayne's mother had contacted Dr Li to express her concern about Wayne's increasingly erratic behaviour, but had asked Dr Li not to let Wayne know she had done so, in case he reacted violently. In this situation, Dr Li would need to make sure that Mrs Morgan's confidentiality was preserved, and would not be free to share this information with Wayne.

Had Wayne wanted to see his social services record, he would legally be in a similar position, but would find that here, too, there were certain exceptions to his right of access (contained in the Data Protection (Subject Access Modification) (Social Work) Order 2000).

Accessibility is not just about whether or not you are allowed to see your records. It also includes consideration of **where** your records are kept – for example, whether you have them at home or whether they are stored by the agency. Generally, records have been banked with the service rather than being placed with the service user. When Wayne requested to see his medical records, he was aware that there was one copy and that this was stored at the surgery. So it would be inaccessible to him without making specific arrangements with Dr Li.

In fact, Dr Li has considered putting all the patient records into an electronic system, but this is likely to make them even more inaccessible to a service user like Wayne who does not own a computer.

In some situations, services users do not need to go to the service provider to ask to see their records, as they hold copies themselves. For example, it is recommended that service users are given written copies of their care plans (Department of Health, 1991a; Northern Ireland Office, 1991). Also, antenatal records, infant care records, home dialysis records and diabetes records are commonly held by the service user or patient. So should more service users hold their own records? Gilhooly and McGhee (1991) summarised the research on patient-held records up to 1991 and Christine Hogg evaluated this in 1994, resulting in Table 2.

Table 2 An evaluation of patient-held records

Against patient-held records	*For patient-held records*
Patients will lose their records	Research shows that records are less likely to be lost if held by patients
GPs will need to spend more time explaining the notes	The benefits of spending more time in explaining outweigh this
The costs of producing and updating double copies, where both are necessary	Not always necessary to keep double copies, or modified form of notes can be provided
GPs will feel restricted and keep another set of private notes – i.e. when patients hold the records GPs won't put the truth in them	A study found that GPs were more likely to 'censor' diagnoses such as obesity than cancer or a terminal illness!
Detailed information makes people more anxious	Studies show that access and possession of records reassures patients
Detailed information destroys the rapport and trust between doctor and patient	Studies show that patient-held records increase the rapport between GP and patient
Records kept at home may be seen by other people without permission of the patient	Patients can control the confidentiality of their own records
	Patients can correct any inaccuracies in their records. Studies show 10–12% errors in patients' notes
	Locums and deputies have access to notes on home visits
	Notes can cover both health and social care and improve co-ordination of services
	No delays when patients move or change GPs
	Savings in storage and retrieval in GP surgery

(Source: adapted from Hogg, 1994, diagram 4, p. 47 (7))

In Table 2 Hogg makes a very good case for patient-held records, and by implication for service user-held records in social care.

Giving service users their own records to keep is one way of solving the problem of people becoming detached from the service records concerning them. But modern information technology suggests other ways. Fax already allows for more rapid transfer of information from one authority to another, so that records can chase people round the country more quickly. Another possibility might be electronic patient records (EPRs) which are now technically feasible (Silicon Bridge Research, 1997). EPRs are not simply records typed into a computer, but records which can be read by the computer so that, on instruction, the computer can search for names, conditions, medications, or kinds of care packages, and can produce summaries, and so on. There are many hospitals in the USA and in continental Europe, and several in the UK (Cross, 1997a) where all patient records made in the hospital are in electronic form. However, at this stage electronic systems are of limited usefulness as not all NHS trusts, health authorities and GPs subscribe to the same Health Information Support System so cannot readily share data.

Modern information technology allows for large amounts of personal information to be stored in tiny microchips, which might be worn as pendants or bracelets, or incorporated into a smart card.

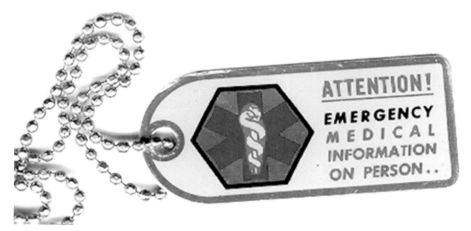

Modern information technology allows for large amounts of personal information to be stored in tiny microchips which might be worn as pendants or bracelets, or incorporated into a small card

Such devices would make it much easier for service users to hold their own records – though they would, of course, be less able to access the information contained there unless they had (and knew how to use) appropriate systems for 'reading' the records. Microchip implants into the patient's body would make it much less likely that people would lose their records, but we might need some persuasion before agreeing to this method of storing information! Electronic and microchip-based information systems may well have some advantages over paper-based storage, but they also have implications for privacy and confidentiality. Once information about a patient is part of a widespread electronic network, there are thousands of different points at which the information can be accessed, legally or illegally – unlike the limited opportunities for this with paper records (Feldbaum and Dick, 1997).

Comprehensible records

The right to see one's own records is now very well established in law, but the records of health and social care are often incomprehensible to non-professionals. People who receive health and social care services are often ill, confused or anxious, and their capacity to understand what is recorded about them may be limited. This is sometimes used as an excuse to withhold most of the documentation from them, unless they specifically ask for it, on the grounds that giving them more information would add to their burden, or that they would not understand the information anyway. But this policy is just as likely to add to their confusion and anxiety as it is to relieve it. Usually it is better to give people information, so that they have a chance to understand it, than to withhold it on the assumption that they will not. This implies giving them the kind of information which they have the best chance of understanding. For people who are literate, written information can be used to support spoken information because they can review it at their own pace and in their own time. Audio or videotaped information or pictograms (see Unit 14) can be used where service users have difficulty with literacy. Interpreters and translators may be necessary where people do not speak English, or have a visual or hearing impairment.

What you read about making information about services more 'user-friendly' in Unit 22 is equally applicable to making records more comprehensible to service users. There is, however, a tension between, on the one hand, making records which economically and efficiently convey perhaps quite technical information to practitioners and, on the other, making records which are comprehensible to service users.

It is not necessary (nor would it be practical) to expect health records to be written entirely in non-technical or 'lay' terminology. *"Professionals need to communicate with other professionals in professional terms."* But steps can be taken to make records more understandable.

> *One suggestion to improve patient/client understanding is a 'patient-friendly' section – i.e. a summary of information previously discussed with the patient/client. As well as [reinforcing] their understanding of discussions, the summary also informs other health professionals what the patient knows about his/her condition, problems and care.*
>
> *(National Health Service Training Directorate, 1995, E6)*

In addition, while such summaries might not answer all the patient's questions, they would put a patient in a much better position to ask questions in future. Other ideas include glossaries explaining abbreviations and technical terms, and diagrams explaining how the body works on which the particular patient's condition can be indicated.

People wanting to find out more about a medical condition which appears in their records can make use of the national Health Information Service: freephone 0800 66 55 44.

As we have seen, issues around access to personal information are complicated as records need to be both accessible and understandable, and this is not always easy to achieve. However, there are examples of innovative practice (e.g. Lindsey and Russell, 1999, p. 4) which show that much can be done to make records more useful and accessible to users of health and social care services.

Key points

- The right to access your own health or social care records is well established in law, although often service users don't seem to know they have these rights.

- Rights to access your own records don't amount to much if you can't understand the records when you look at them.

1.4 Involving service users in making records

Service users and informal carers supply workers with a great deal of information, edited versions of which subsequently appear in the records. For example, renal (kidney failure) patients may be asked to keep a record of their food and fluid intake. Parents may be asked to complete records of a child's progress on a programme designed to remedy bed-wetting. In the same kind of programme the child may be involved in recording by sticking stars on his or her own continence chart. Depression management programmes and programmes for dealing with panic attacks often entail diaries kept by the client and self-assessment forms filled in by the client periodically (see the example overleaf). Applications for most welfare benefits are records, which are usually filled in by applicants themselves. So also are 'customer satisfaction' questionnaires and complaints forms.

Conditions for service users to make records

Involving service users in making their own records is a way of recognising their knowledge about their own situations and ensuring that their voices are properly incorporated into any plans or decisions made about them. In some situations, records may need to be quite technical. For example, some of those most likely to hold and make entries into their own records include patients and carers who carry out home dialysis, and people with diabetes who manage their own medication and who test and record their own blood sugar levels. Both these groups have to receive training to manage their own care and to record it appropriately. Greater involvement in record making teaches clients skills they can use in self-assertion and self-care but it may also require training so that they know how to recognise what is relevant and recordable.

Diary Sheet

Please make an entry whenever you notice a definite increase in anxiety

Date/time	Description of situation	Anxiety level: 0–10	Description of (a) physical feelings (b) thoughts	Coping method	Anxiety level after: 0–10

© T. Powell, 1992. You may photocopy this page for instructional use only.

20

A diary of anxiety levels. Sometimes service users are the best people to make records about themselves. This may be when the information is about their feelings, which they know best about, or when they are out of contact with practitioners. Making a record yourself helps you learn about yourself

While most users of services might be expected to be honest and accurate in making their own records, there are those who are not. Pat Walsh's husband has been a patient at the renal unit for some months. In renal units, where people come for kidney dialysis, a major problem is that patients often eat and drink a great deal more between dialysis sessions than they include in their records. For some, it is a chore to have to record everything eaten or drunk – and to have to do this reliably week in, week out. But perhaps more importantly, patients may have suspicions, not entirely unfounded, that those who stick to their diets and fluid regimes are those who will be selected for transplants or home dialysis, so they have some very good reasons for lying (Gomm,

1989). But it is difficult for clinicians to make judgements about treatment when they cannot be certain if patients are telling the truth. And it can also affect the development of good relationships if nurses are faced with patients who are obviously lying to them in presenting their self-completed dietary records.

So should patients like Mr Walsh be asked to keep their own record of their diet and fluid intake between visits to the renal unit? *If this can be done safely,* it is better to treat Mr Walsh as trustworthy even if he might not be, rather than treat him as untrustworthy when he might be completely honest. The safety issue in this case cannot be managed by finding another way of recording diet and fluid intake between visits to the unit. At home, what patients eat and drink has to be recorded by someone there. Nurses wish from time to time that his wife could do the recording, but recognise that this would discourage him from taking responsibility for himself (Gomm, 1989). But the clinical staff need to make an accurate assessment of Mr Walsh's current condition, so they will need to look for other sources of information to place alongside the food diary that he has completed. In this way, the information that Mr Walsh supplies is only part of the picture and clinic staff will be able to add other pieces to the jigsaw through the weighing and other examinations done before Mr Walsh is put on the dialysis machines. Given these safety measures, the risk of him falsifying his record sheets is worth taking in an attempt to get him to take more responsibility for his own care.

Under other circumstances, though, it may simply be too unsafe to do this. For example, in prescribing methadone and other drugs for Michelle to manage her heroin addiction Dr Li will ask her about her recent drug-taking behaviour. But in addition, Dr Li is likely to require that Michelle has a urine test, to ensure that she has independent information about Michelle's heroin use. The reason for this is that safe prescribing for people addicted to opiates requires precise information about recent drug-taking behaviour. Prescribing on the basis of self-recording (or self-reports) is just too risky for most doctors to contemplate (Waller, 1993).

It is important to remember that some people are too ill or confused to make their own records; and that not all clients wanting to use services would be happy about assessing their own needs and making their own plans, participating in their own treatments and recording all this, even if someone helped them with the recording.

Key points

- When service users are allowed to make entries into their own records this may give them an opportunity to record what they think is important to them, and it includes them as 'partners in care'.

- Service users and informal carers may need some training if they are to be involved in making entries into the records of health and social care, but this will enhance their ability to make decisions for themselves and care for themselves.

- There are limits of capability, expertise and trustworthiness, and considerations of safety which may put limits on how far service users can contribute to their own records.

Section 2
Who controls information and how?

So far we have looked at recording information as a practical matter of writing down whatever might be useful. But is it always a good idea to let people record information about you? And, whether is it or not, do you have any choice?

2.1 Privacy or disclosure: who decides?

Do would-be users of services have a real choice about what information they give away about themselves?

Whatever the service, there is a minimum amount of information which a user has to disclose *as a condition* for receiving the service. Thus the doctor might say to the patient, 'Unless you drop your trousers I can't do any more about the pain in your groin.' The counsellor might say to the client, 'I respect your right to privacy but if you are not going to disclose your feelings to me, then it's not worth us continuing this counselling relationship.' The Benefits Agency official might say to the claimant, 'Unless you can provide me with evidence that you are not engaged in paid work I can't go on authorising your income support.' In this sense, although clients have a choice, it is only the choice between disclosing and receiving the service, and not disclosing and not receiving the service.

Many service users find practitioners' questions offensive. This raises the question of whether practitioners need to ask certain questions, and if they ask them whether they should record the answers.

Activity 3   **Intrusion or the need to know**

Allow about 15 minutes   For this activity read the following scenario. It is based on a real example (Valios, 1996, p.9). Consider (a) whether the social services department needed to know this information and (b) if they did need to know it whether they needed to record it.

Mr Thomas Li recently had a fall, which resulted in a broken hip. He had surgery to replace the hip and was subsequently discharged back home. He still has some difficulty getting around, and uses a walking frame. Prior to the accident, he was managing to look after himself with some support from a home carer. However, since coming home, he seems to have lost confidence and has also been complaining that his sight has become worse, making it harder for him to cope. Dev Sharma suggested that he could benefit from attending a local rehabilitation day centre and arranged for him to visit for an assessment. Mr Li went once and refused to go back, saying that the staff had asked him all sorts of questions that he found insulting and offensive. He was asked about personal hygiene, whether he could get himself dressed, and manage to get on and off the toilet by himself. In addition, he was asked about his financial situation; as he said to Dev Sharma, "they wanted to

> know all my personal business and would not stop asking me questions about how much money I had".

Comment (a) Need to know

Abilities in personal care. Given that this is a rehabilitation centre whose task is to help users to improve their daily living skills, it does seem important that staff know what users can do, and how much their abilities change over time. Asking service users for their views on this seems rather better than staff recording such matters without asking.

Financial situation. Given that central government allocates finances to social services departments on the assumption that they will raise income from charging for services such as this, and that charges should be levied according to ability to pay, it does seem as if the council needs to have this information if it is likely to levy charges in the future.

(b) Need to record

Abilities in personal care. If providing a service were just a matter between a worker and a service user then perhaps there would be no need to record this information. But recording allows for continuity of care. Moreover, this is a publicly funded service, so it has to be accountable for providing appropriate services to people who have a need for them and benefit from them. It is difficult to see how it could be accountable without recording service users' abilities and progress.

Financial situation. The only way in which a social services department can demonstrate that it is levying charges according to its own scheme of charging is to make records of the financial circumstances of the service users and of the fees they are charged.

From the scenario it is not clear exactly how the questions were asked. Mr Li may have felt uncomfortable being asked personal questions by a female worker at the centre, and in many cultures it would be considered extremely rude to ask about personal finances. He may also have preferred to have this sensitive conversation in his first language (Cantonese) rather than English. But so long as you accept that the task of this day centre is to facilitate the development of daily living skills, then you have to accept that staff need to know what skills the centre users have. How could staff do their jobs otherwise? You might object to charges being made, but if they are to be made, then asking questions about income seems inevitable. Perhaps the most important point, however, is that publicly funded services are not private matters between a service user and a service. It is not like using a private gym for which the users pay themselves. These are public services and have to be publicly accountable, as noted above. On the issue of personal living skills, centre staff probably made records even though Mr Li didn't answer the questions himself, and probably less accurately than he would have done. On the issue of finance Mr Li has a choice. If he doesn't disclose his financial situation and the social services department levies charges, he will be billed at the highest rate. There is some evidence that some service users choose not to use services rather than disclose their financial circumstances (Dobson, 1996).

In this case, Dev was able to spend time with Mr Li explaining why the different sorts of information were required. He also confirmed that Mr

Li felt awkward talking to a young woman about personal matters. As a result of this, the centre manager set up another meeting for Mr Li with a male colleague; Mr Li, in turn, was reassured about the purpose of the different questions and felt able to supply enough information to allow for a proper assessment.

Sometimes service users have virtually no choice but to disclose information. For example, pre-sentence reports (PSRs) are completed by probation officers to aid the court in deciding an appropriate sentence. The offender can refuse to co-operate in this, but in doing so would be passing over an opportunity to influence the sentence.

By contrast there are some services which require very little disclosure from their clients at all. These include the services of the Samaritans (which are available to people who remain anonymous), night shelters and other facilities for the homeless, and the services of needle and syringe exchanges which routinely and knowingly deal with people who give false names for the records such exchanges have to keep.

Key point

- For many health or social care services there is a minimum of information which clients are required to disclose as a condition for receiving the service.

2.2 Managing privacy: confidentiality and consent

Health and social care work records are rarely just made as an *aide-mémoire* for the person who makes them. Although some counsellors and psychotherapists in private practice keep records which are only accessible to themselves and the client concerned, most records in health and care are made with a view to the information in them being shared. This allows continuity of care if individual practitioners become sick, go on holiday or change their jobs. Records allow successors, colleagues and locums to pick up where another left off. Records are also an important facility for co-ordinating care when different practitioners in a range of agencies need to share some of the same information. However, sharing the information in records raises issues about whom the information should be shared with, what they may or may not do with it, and what rights clients have to know how and with whom information about themselves is likely to be shared.

Implicit consent

Whether they realise it or not, when patients tell something to a doctor they are authorising the sharing of that information with the doctor's colleagues and secretaries, records clerks and managers in the same agency, and perhaps with a range of people in other agencies as well. This is because the NHS operates the rather paradoxical doctrine of *implicit consent*. It is paradoxical because it is a way of giving consent without giving consent. Unless patients specifically ask otherwise, they are deemed to have consented to the information they have given to one practitioner in the service being shared with others.

Implicit consent

Unless they specifically state otherwise it is assumed that service users have given 'implicit consent' to:

- the transfer of information given to one practitioner within the NHS to other practitioners involved in the patient's care

- the transfer of information held within the NHS to social services involved in the patient's care.

A patient who is unable to give informed consent is deemed to have given implicit consent to actions which are performed in his or her own interests.

The doctrine of implicit consent should not be over-used. It is good practice to ask for explicit consent.

When acting on 'implicit consent' practitioners have a duty of care to ensure that information is only shared with those who:

- have a legitimate right to know

- can be trusted to act in the patient's interests or, failing that, the public interest

- can be trusted not to disclose the information improperly.

(Adapted from Department of Health, 1996c, OHT29)

From this box you will see that there are some very good reasons why the doctrine of implicit consent is necessary. It refers to 'a patient who is unable to give informed consent'. This includes people who are unconscious, or very agitated or confused. It would obviously be impossible to run health and social services if no information could be transferred before an unconscious patient regained consciousness, or unless a person with Alzheimer's disease became lucid enough to be asked permission. In strictly legal terms the extent to which an adult person's 'next of kin' can give consent to the transfer of information about their relative is a rather cloudy area, but the idea of implicit consent makes seeking such permission unnecessary. In addition, however capable the person might be, it would make health services very difficult to run if consent was required for each and every occasion that records passed from person to person: hospital doctors, social workers, medical students, general practitioners, medical records officers, chaplains, secretaries, ward clerks, radiographers, pharmacists, practice managers, locums, agency staff, and so on.

However, as it says in the box, it is considered good practice to ask for explicit consent whenever this is possible:

> 3.1 *All NHS bodies must have an active policy for informing patients of the kind of purposes for which information about them is collected and categories of people or organisations to which information may need to be passed.*

(Department of Health, 1996a, p. 7)

Explicit consent

Although social services and social work departments and other agencies in the health and social field often seem to behave as if they had policies of implicit consent, in fact they do not. Hence the well-run agency will seek explicit consent for information about service users to be shared within the agency concerned, and perhaps more widely, as the example shows.

Other Agencies Involved	Contact Name	Tel. No.	Date

CLIENT INFORMATION SHARING AGREEMENT

I agree that the details contained in this assessment can be shared with other agencies involved in my care.

Client/Patient signature

Date

Some social services departments make it clear to service users that information about them will be shared within the agency and sometimes beyond. This example is based on forms used by Kent County Council

The idea of explicit consent implies that the person gives consent, knowing exactly what they are agreeing to – informed explicit consent. This suggests that agencies should take care to explain the implications of divulging information to the person who is asked for it. As with other kinds of communication discussed earlier, this explanation needs to be in terms understandable to service users, answering the questions they need answered.

Earlier in this unit it was suggested that it is important to keep the recording of information to the minimum necessary. The reason given then was in terms of the costs of collecting and curating information. But considerations of confidentiality lead to the same conclusion. The difficulty, as always, is deciding what is the minimum necessary.

Key points

- Best practice is always to make efforts to explain to service users what information collected about them will be used for, and with whom it is likely to be shared.

- This puts them in a position to give explicit and informed consent or to decide against providing the information.

- Sometimes, however, the service user may not be in a position to consent. Then decisions have to be taken by others with the service user's best interests in mind.

Section 3
The duty of confidentiality

Once we accept that health and social care agencies need to store personal information about us, a new issue arises: confidentiality. Information contained in service users' records is often personal and may be highly sensitive – the sorts of things you may not want other people to know about you without good reason. So policies and procedures for maintaining **confidentiality** will then be necessary. In this section, therefore, we look at how confidentiality can be managed.

3.1 Enforcing confidentiality

We can see that confidentiality is a major issue in care services simply by looking at the number of devices used in attempting to enforce it. They include the following.

- Agency confidentiality policies (you will look at one of these shortly).

- Contracts of employment in which failure to follow the agency confidentiality policy can be a dismissible offence.

- Complaints procedures which allow clients who feel that their confidentiality has been breached to complain about the person concerned (e.g. Department of Health, 1995c; National Health Service Executive, 1996a).

- Professional codes of conduct. Those practitioners who are members of professional associations, such as doctors, nurses, chiropodists or occupational therapists, are bound by codes of conduct which always include clauses on maintaining confidentiality and not taking advantage of confidential information. Breaching such codes can lead to disciplinary action by the professional association, and might lead to the person being struck from the professional register and hence being unable to continue to practise (e.g. General Medical Council, 1993; Nursing and Midwifery Council, 2002).

- Laws requiring organisations to protect confidential information. The most important of these are the Data Protection Act 1998 and the Freedom of Information Act 2000.

- The civil law gives people who believe their confidentiality has been breached the opportunity to sue for damages – but only if they can demonstrate that some tangible harm has come to them in consequence.

- International treaty obligations, such as the European Convention on Human Rights, also guarantee privacy and confidentiality. You will be looking at this in Section 4.

In spite of all these structures, confidentiality is not always easy to maintain. Confidentiality, with regard to gossip or records, can be particularly difficult in agencies with informal styles of working and where 'workers' may be volunteers, without the contracts of employment or membership of professional associations which can be used to discipline paid workers. One approach to this is to avoid recording personal details almost entirely (as the mental health charity MIND advises: Villeneau, 1994). But when voluntary organisations take on contracts, this usually involves them in recording information about service users (National Health Service Executive, 1995).

Anyone who works in the NHS or in a local authority social services or social work department will know that they can be rather 'leaky' so far as confidentiality is concerned. Many people who work there simply do discuss patients or clients with their spouses and their friends, even if they usually try to do so without identifying them. However, such breaches of confidentiality do not usually concern what is written into the records. More usually the breaches come from the everyday chat of working life. By comparison with gossip, the confidentiality of records is relatively easy to ensure. Because records are physical objects they can be locked away, or, if electronic, can be protected with passwords and security codes or by encryption. In the last resort it is impossible to defeat a determined hacker, but it is possible to make unauthorised access difficult (Feldbaum and Dick, 1997).

Activity 4   **How much harm does it do?**

Allow about 10 minutes   At first sight it may not seem to be too serious a matter if someone's private affairs become known by outsiders to the health and care services, particularly if they don't know that they are being talked about behind their back. But think about the kind of information that somebody like Pat Walsh has access to, through her role as Dr Li's receptionist. Jot down some ideas about when such a breach of confidentiality might be seriously harmful to someone.

Comment   Once information is outside the group of people who are bound by a confidentiality policy there is no knowing where it might get to, or how distorted it might become in the retelling. Some kinds of information can be very stigmatising, for example information that someone has had a test for HIV or has attended a clinic for sexually transmitted diseases, has had an appointment with a psychiatrist, or has attended Alcoholics Anonymous. If that person's partner doesn't know and gets to hear about it on the grapevine, it won't bode well for their relationship. If a current or prospective employer gets to know, it might ruin someone's job prospects. Sometimes records contain information about illegitimate children that a person wants kept confidential from a current partner, or past criminal offences, or information that they were themselves adopted, or that they had a sex change operation, and so on and so on. Some confidential information has a commercial value. Examples include medical information, information from genetic testing which is of interest to insurance companies and any information about celebrities which will be of interest to the media. And of course, there is always the possibility of blackmail.

> **Key points**
> *   There are many devices for enforcing confidentiality including agency codes, employment contracts, professional codes of practice and parliamentary and EU legislation.
> *   In spite of confidentiality policies, health and social care agencies are often 'leaky', particularly with regard to gossip.

3.2 Professional codes of confidentiality

Privacy and confidentiality always feature in the lists of values subscribed to by professionals involved in health and social care – and by many others as well, such as lawyers, accountants and the clergy. Nearly everyone who works in a health or social care context works in an organisation which has a written confidentiality policy, or belongs to an occupational group which has its own code of practice. Serious and unjustifiable breaches of confidentiality by professionals can lead to their being struck off the professional register.

In the box below, we have printed an extract from the professional code of conduct for nurses.

---

5. As a registered nurse or midwife, you must protect confidential information.

5.1 You must treat information about patients and clients as confidential and use it only for the purposes for which it was given. As it is impractical to obtain consent every time you need to share information with others, you should ensure that patients and clients understand that some information may be made available to other members of the team involved in the delivery of care. You must guard against breaches of confidentiality by protecting information from improper disclosure at all times.

5.2 You should seek patients' and clients' wishes regarding the sharing of information with their family and others. When a patient or client is considered incapable of giving permission, you should consult relevant colleagues.

5.3 If you are required to disclose information outside the team that will have personal consequences for patients or clients, you must obtain their consent. If the patient or client withholds consent, or if consent cannot be obtained for whatever reason, disclosures may be made only where:
   - they can be justified in the public interest (usually where disclosure is essential to protect the patient or client or someone else from the risk of significant harm)
   - they are required by law or by order of a court.

5.4 Where there is an issue of child protection, you must act at all times in accordance with national and local policies.

(Nursing and Midwifery Council (2000), Code of Professional Conduct, clause 5)

Confidentiality is also one of the fundamental values which is assessed in VQ schemes in health and social care. The next box quotes from the revised Level 3 VQ in care as current in 1998.

Confidentiality in a VQ scheme

02.3   Promote people's right to the confidentiality of information

Performance criteria

(1)   <u>information stored</u> in, and retrieved from, recording systems is consistent with the requirements of legislation and organisational policy

(2)   records made by the worker are accurate and legible and only contain the information necessary for the record's purpose

(3)   information is only disclosed to those who have the right and the need to know once proof of identity has been obtained

(4)   the <u>appropriate precautions</u> are taken when <u>communicating</u> confidential or sensitive information to those who have the right and need to know it

(5)   when someone tells the worker something which the worker is required to share with others, the person is clearly told in an appropriate manner that the information may need to be shared with others

(6)   confidential records are handled securely and stored in the correct place

(7)   <u>support</u> is sought by the worker when it appears that information is being misused.

(CCETSW/City and Guilds, 1997, p. 8)

(For more detail about the assessment of competence in VQ schemes see Getting a Vocational Qualification: A Student's Guide.)

Such policies or codes are sometimes difficult to apply to particular circumstances. But they do reduce the number of occasions when workers find it difficult to know what to do. Because of such policies and codes, much confidentiality practice is a matter of following printed rules. The skill then is in working out how the rules apply in particular situations.

Confidentiality policies quite rightly differ from agency to agency, because different agencies have a 'need to know' different kinds of information, and because different agencies are confronted with different challenges in trying to keep information confidential. Since the 'right answers' on confidentiality differ from agency to agency, we are going to look at how the confidentiality policy works in NIAS, the fictitious drug agency in Unit 22, attended by Michelle and Wayne.

3.3 Introducing an agency and its confidentiality policy

Narcotics Information and Advice Service

The Narcotics Information and Advice Service (NIAS) is a 'street' drugs agency. Staff at NIAS work closely with the drug problem team (DPT) in the local NHS trust, which is the main prescriber of methadone (the drug prescribed as a legal alternative to heroin). Not all NIAS clients are clients of the DPT, and not all DPT clients are in contact with NIAS. Workers at NIAS attend the weekly meetings of the DPT, where decisions are made on whether cases should be dealt with by NIAS, or by one of the community addiction nurses, or both. Matters discussed at the DPT meetings are covered by both the NIAS and the NHS trust confidentiality policies.

NIAS has seven permanent staff and a number of sessional workers. It has a team of volunteers who usually befriend one or more clients. Pat Walsh, from the Grove Health Centre, has been a volunteer with the agency for about two years. NIAS is a company limited by guarantee and a charity, and has an unpaid management committee elected at a public annual general meeting. Most of its funding comes from contracts with the health authority and the local authority social services department. Both scrutinised the NIAS confidentiality policy and checked it against their own criteria for contractors' confidentiality policies as a condition of awarding the contracts.

NIAS maintains two offices five days a week in two inner-city London boroughs and satellite offices one day a week each in two outer-London areas. The two full-time offices have an appointments-only system in the mornings, a drop-in service in the afternoons, and one late-night opening in each office. Workers and volunteers also visit people in their homes and in prison.

Activity 5   **Introducing NIAS**

Allow about 15 minutes   Having read the sketch of the agency, jot down your initial thoughts about the kinds of information which might be 'sensitive', and which NIAS will be particularly concerned to keep confidential.

Comment   There is no comment following this activity. Instead, the activities which follow cover many of the more sensitive kinds of information.

The confidentiality policy

In this unit we will be looking at how the policy works and the kinds of practical and ethical issues that arise when you try and implement it. So first of all, turn to the Offprint Book, p. 126 and quickly read through the policy to get a rough idea of the areas it covers. You don't have to remember the details and will be able to refer back to the policy at different points in the later activities.

Activity 6   **Getting to know the policy**

Allow about 15 minutes   To start focusing on the policy, go back and read through the first four clauses and answer the following questions:

(i)   Why does NIAS think it is important to have a confidentiality policy?

(ii)   Can an employee be dismissed for breach of confidentiality? Can a volunteer?

(iii)   Who is covered by the policy?

(iv)   Can an employee or volunteer use information about a service user if that information was obtained through work in another agency?

(v)   Can employees/volunteers share information freely about service users?

Comment   (i)   This is answered in the preamble to clause 1: the policy is important because it assures service users that they can trust the agency. Without this, it would be impossible to run the service.

(ii)   Yes. Clause 1 states that both employees and volunteers can be dismissed for breach of confidentiality.

(iii)   All clients of the service are covered. Clause 2 defines who 'a client' is, for the purposes of the policy.

(iv)   No, such information should generally not be used. The only exception, as stated in clause 3, is if non-disclosure would pose a serious risk to health or safety.

(v)   No. Information about service users should only be shared within the agency on a 'need-to-know' basis (clause 4). Clause 4 also says that information will only be shared outside the agency under certain conditions (set out later in clause 5).

The activities in the rest of this section are designed to give you practice in interpreting a confidentiality policy and thinking about the practical and ethical issues that can arise. We will concentrate on different situations in which information about service users may need to be shared beyond the agency.

3.4 Applying the policy: disclosure beyond the agency

The NIAS confidentiality policy is quite a long document as it has to cover different situations where staff or volunteers might have to share information about service users with other agencies. You may notice that clauses 5 to 11, 13 (and 16 and 20) all relate to transfers of information from NIAS to other agencies. That's nearly half the policy. Figure 1 gives you a picture of the kinds of transfer which might be made, with or without the client's consent, from an agency such as NIAS.

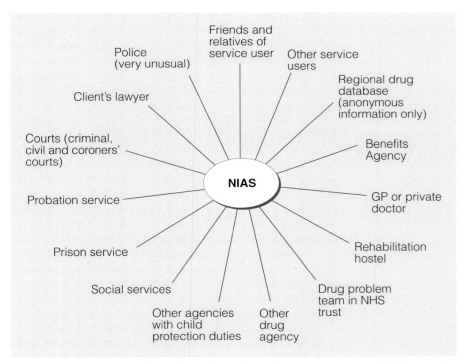

Figure 1 Other agencies and people to whom it may be necessary to transfer information about NIAS clients, with or without their consent

The activities in the remainder of this section all focus on requests for information about NIAS clients from outside the agency, and draw on information in clauses 1-14 of the policy. The activities relate to the series of case studies below. You have already met Wayne Morgan and Michelle McDonald, but here is some additional information about them and about one of their friends who also uses NIAS. For these activities, imagine that you are either a member of staff or a volunteer at NIAS.

Jonti

Jonti, a friend of Wayne's, is a 25-year-old drug user who is being prescribed methadone by the drug problem team of the NHS trust. NIAS is working with Jonti to help him sort out various aspects of his life, such as accommodation and personal relationships. Thus he is a client of both the drug problem team and of NIAS. Jonti has signed a consent form agreeing to NIAS discussing his affairs at drug problem team meetings where a consultant psychiatrist, community addiction nurses, a clinical psychologist and a hospital social worker will be present, as well as NIAS staff. You have reason to believe that Jonti is taking heroin in addition to his methadone. When you confront Jonti with this, he admits it but asks you not to tell the consultant, since this information may lead to his methadone prescription being withdrawn.

Michelle

Michelle is a heroin user and a client of NIAS. She has an 18-month-old daughter, Sarah. A social worker from the child protection team telephones NIAS and asks you whether you can supply any information relevant to a case conference which will be held next week to consider whether to take Michelle's child into care. Michelle has not given any consent to her affairs being discussed with social services.

Wayne

Wayne is a client of NIAS and the drug problem team. He is a heavy user of amphetamine sulphate ('speed') which causes him to behave in ways that other people find bizarre. You are telephoned by an approved social worker (ASW), who tells you the following. Wayne's mother can no longer tolerate his behaviour and has asked for him to be detained in hospital under the Mental Health Act 1983 (England and Wales). Wayne has barricaded himself in the house and the police have been called to use their powers under the Mental Health Act (Section 136) to remove him to 'a place of safety'. In such circumstances an ASW is usually asked to attend. The ASW wants to know if Wayne is a drug user. People can be detained under the Mental Health Act only if they are suffering from a mental disorder. Being 'high' on amphetamine sulphate is not a mental disorder for the purpose of the Act. You are in a position to supply information which might prevent Wayne from being forcibly detained in an acute psychiatric ward. Wayne has not given any consent for his affairs to be discussed with social services.

Activity 7   Interpreting the policy on disclosure

Allow about 25 minutes   For each case study decide and note down what you think the NIAS confidentiality policy says that you should do. (Though you would, of course, want to make sure that the Director supported any decision you proposed, as outlined in clause 7.)

Do the activity in two stages. First read each case and note down which clauses of the confidentiality policy are most relevant to it. Then, using the relevant clauses, decide what should be done.

Comment   The first case, that of **Jonti**, differs from the others since he has given permission for information about his drug-taking behaviour to be disclosed – in this case to the drug problem team. Now he wants to go back on that undertaking. He is explicitly instructing you not to disclose this new information, so clause 5(a) no longer applies. Clause 5(b) lists the conditions under which you can disclose information without the client's consent. None of these apply to Jonti, so the policy forces you to do what he asks. However, doing this means that, as far as Jonti is concerned, you can no longer work in partnership with the drug problem team. To continue as before, but behaving at drug problem team meetings as if you did not know that Jonti was taking heroin in addition to his methadone prescription, would be dishonest. You may feel that you have to tell the team that the situation has changed and that you no longer have Jonti's permission to share information about his drug use. And of course, the team may well guess what is going on if you suddenly refuse to share information about Jonti with them. Did anyone warn Jonti that once he had given consent, withdrawing it could have this effect?

The other cases all involve telephone contacts, so you would first need to consider the authenticity of the callers. Clause 9(i) states, 'the credentials of those who will receive the information should be verified if there is any doubt about them'. How do you know whether the caller is really the person they say they are?

Neither of these clients has given consent, so clause 5(b) of the policy applies. There are three sub-clauses of clause 5(b) which might provide a justification for releasing information without the client's consent.

> *Information should be transferred ... only in the following circumstances:*
>
> *(i) when disclosure is required by a warrant or a court order; and/or*
>
> *(ii) when non-disclosure would pose a serious risk to:*
>
> > *– the welfare of a child*
> >
> > *– the safety of an employee, a volunteer, another client, or some other person; and/or*
>
> *(iii) where the client is not in a position to give consent. If neither (i) nor (ii) above apply, then information may be released on an estimation of the client's best interests alone.*

For **Michelle** there is an opportunity for NIAS to ask her whether she would like information to be released about her, and if so what information (see clause 6). Indeed it is common practice for drug agencies to contribute to different sorts of report, for example pre-sentence reports or reports to child protection case conferences, and information is not necessarily restricted to what the client has agreed to – you will look at that in the next activity.

By contrast, **Wayne's** situation is pressing and immediate. There is no time to ask for his consent, so the relevant clause of the policy is 5b(iii). Barricaded in his room, in imminent danger of being compulsorily removed from home, Wayne is in no position to give consent. So the question is whether it is in Wayne's best interests to release or withhold the information, always assuming that the credentials of the ASW can be verified. That's a matter for professional judgement, but the situation suggests disclosure under clause 5b(iii). The ASW will still have to decide whether (1) Wayne's behaviour is caused by the recent ingestion or injection of amphetamine sulphate or another drug – and that his behaviour is not a mental disorder, or (2) his behaviour is due to the long-term damage of taking drugs – drug-induced psychosis – which is a mental disorder for the purpose of the Mental Health Act. As an NIAS worker you will be thankful you don't have to make such decisions.

If you disclose this information about Wayne you will also have to record it (clause 11) and report this disclosure without consent to the NIAS management committee (clause 7) (although without identifying Wayne to them, as you will see when you come to read clause 17).

However, Wayne is also a client of the drug problem team. If the ASW telephoned them, and established her credentials, they would give her the information with far less hesitation than would NIAS. To understand this you might like to look back at the box on page 67 which outlines the doctrine of implicit consent.

The comment above didn't deal fully with Michelle. You will consider her further in the next activity, but first read the following background information.

You have refused to give information about Michelle over the phone, but you call round to see her at home.

More about Michelle

You've been worried about Michelle's daughter Sarah for some time, although until now your concerns have largely arisen from things she's let slip or things said by other clients – mainly about Michelle leaving Sarah to the care of other drug users for long periods of time. The actions of the child protection team have brought matters to a head. Your visit to Michelle increases your concerns. The flat is dirty and there are dirty needles in places where Sarah might get at them. Michelle wants you to speak on her behalf at the case conference which will decide whether her child should be taken into care or not, saying how well she looks after Sarah.

Activity 8   **Disclosure against the service user's wishes**

Allow about 25 minutes   What does the confidentiality policy suggest you should do in this case?

Look first at clause 8 of the policy and decide how that might apply here.

In this case you have four options:

(1)   give only information that is agreed with the client

(2)   give some information agreed with the client, and some without the client's consent

(3)   give information even though the client has not consented to any
      information being given

(4)   give no information at all.

Which do you think is the appropriate option here?

Comment   (a)   Clause 8 of the policy says:

*care should be taken to ensure that [information] is accurate and/or
the status of the information is indicated.*

There are two ways of following this instruction. A very strict reading
would mean only transferring information which you were <u>absolutely
certain</u> was true – facts, not opinions. A less strict reading would
allow you to express opinions, but always indicating that they were
opinions. It is worth noting, however, that even when people clearly
state that something is just their opinion, this can be as influential as
what they describe as a 'fact'.

Applied to this case, clause 8 raises the question of what NIAS really
knows for sure about Michelle. For example, you know for sure that
there were dirty needles in reach of a toddler on the occasion of the
visit, but only by hearsay that Michelle leaves Sarah with her drug-
using friends.

(b)   Agencies, including drug agencies, differ in the degree to which they
consider themselves as advocates for service users. Those most
firmly committed to advocacy might take the line that they will
disclose only information that is to the advantage of their client –
provided that withholding other information does no serious harm to
anyone else.

No reputable agency will tell lies on behalf of its clients and on some
occasions there is only a fine line between telling merely half the
truth and telling lies. (And remember that if you were being asked to
make a report to a court, the law of perjury would apply.) In addition,
a very brief report may give rise to a suspicion that something
discreditable to the service user is being withheld.

In Michelle's case, your decision will need to centre on the welfare of
her child. Clause 5b(ii) does allow you to take options (2) or (3):

*Information should be transferred beyond the agency without the
client's explicit consent only in the following circumstances:*

[...]

(ii) when non-disclosure would pose a serious risk to:

   – the welfare of a child

But again whether you would do so would depend on whether the
philosophy of NIAS was primarily to advocate on behalf of its clients,
or whether it saw its duty of care more broadly to give an equal
priority to the welfare of clients' children. You might choose option (4)
(say nothing) on the grounds that the welfare of the child was already
being dealt with by other agencies, and that you had nothing to
contribute which they couldn't find out themselves. Or you might
choose options (2) or (3) (disclosing some information without
consent), on the grounds that NIAS has a definite duty of care
towards the children of service users. In Michelle's case the child
protection team were already involved. But sometimes agencies such
as NIAS are the first to suspect that the welfare of a child may be at

risk. Then they have to make a decision whether to convey their worries to child protection agencies. You can consider this kind of decision in Activity 9.

Activity 9 **Should we alert the child protection team?**

Allow about 20 minutes Suppose that no-one in the statutory health or social services knows about Michelle and Sarah's situation. Only NIAS has seen that there is some cause for concern. What steps does the policy suggest you should take in this case and what other actions do you think would be appropriate?

Note: Some drug agencies receiving some of their funding from social services have a contractual obligation to report children who might be 'at risk'. That means they could lose their funding if they don't. For this activity assume that NIAS has no such contractual obligation.

Comment This question goes a little beyond confidentiality practice, but we can work in the spirit of the policy and see what other actions it suggests the agency might take.

You may have proposed something like this. If NIAS is concerned about the welfare of Michelle's child, it should raise the issue with her and try to work with her to provide a safer environment for the child, for example, in relation to the safe management of needles and drugs in the home. At the same time, however, the confidentiality policy implies (clause 5b(ii)) that NIAS will alert child protection if it feels that Michelle's behaviour continues to put her child at risk. Michelle should be told this (clause 6), and you should act on it if circumstances warrant it. It may be that Michelle can be persuaded herself to approach social services or health visitors for assistance in childcare. However, recommending that she does so depends on a careful estimation of what they are likely to do, and whether it will be to Michelle and/or Sarah's advantage.

Since you have now done a lot of thinking about Michelle and Sarah, it is worth exploring the implications of the policy if the worst happened in this case.

Activity 10 **Legal requirements to disclose**

Allow about 10 minutes Social services have not been involved. NIAS has been working with Michelle to try to minimise the risks to her child. But Sarah eats some tranquilliser tablets. According to Michelle, these were left lying around unbeknown to her by a visitor to her flat. Sarah dies. An inquest is convened. You are called to give evidence. What does the policy say about disclosing information in court?

Comment Actually, it doesn't matter what the policy says. If the court requires you to give evidence then you have a choice between giving evidence or being punished for contempt of court, and between answering the questions asked of you honestly, or risking being found guilty of perjury. Half-truths can count as perjury or as 'obstructing the course of justice'.

If the policy asked you to do otherwise it could not be binding and you could not be dismissed from your job for giving evidence in court despite clause 1. Nor would it be any defence in court to say that you were bound by the agency policy not to disclose any information. However, the policy does actually accord with the law (clause 5b(i)) while clause 8 suggests that in court you should try to stick to the facts and as far as possible avoid being drawn into expressing unsubstantiated opinions.

Key points

- Confidentiality codes and policies are not always easy to apply and can raise complex ethical and practical issues.

- While good practice obliges the worker to observe confidentiality, there are some circumstances where disclosure is necessary.

- A legal requirement to disclose information will override agency policy.

Section 4
Confidentiality, co-ordination and the public interest

As we have seen, there are situations in which the argument for disclosing confidential information is more persuasive than the argument for keeping it confidential. This section discusses such situations further.

4.1 Overriding rights to confidentiality

Like all rights, the rights to privacy and confidentiality are conditional. People have such rights only if they satisfy certain conditions. This is quite clear in the major body of law guaranteeing civil rights in Britain, the European Convention on Human Rights. Britain is a signatory to this convention which has been part of British law since October 2000.

The Convention covers both privacy and confidentiality in Article 8. This says:

> ### Article 8
> 1   *Everyone has the right to respect for his/her private and family life, his/her home and correspondence.*
>
> 2   *There shall be no interference by a public authority with the exercise of this right except in accordance with the law and as is necessary in a democratic society in the interests of national security, public safety, or the economic well being of the country, for the prevention of disorder or crime, or the protection of health or morals, or for the assertion of the rights and freedoms of others.*
>
> *(European Convention on Human Rights Article 8, in Brownlie, 1983, p. 246)*

We see in this statement that there are 'exceptions' to the right to confidentiality, but a lot seems to depend on who defines what is 'necessary', what is 'disorder', what is 'moral', and so on. And this is not entirely a matter for a national government to decide. On several occasions in the 1980s and 1990s the European Court of Human Rights overruled the British Government's definition of such terms. On the whole the European Court is most interested in striking a balance between one individual's right to privacy and the benefits to others of the information not remaining private.

Activity 11   **Exceptions to the right to privacy and confidentiality**

Allow about 10 minutes   Look again at the quotation from Article 8 of the European Convention on Human Rights. You will see that it first grants 'everyone' these rights, and then allows some people's rights to privacy and confidentiality to be overridden by other considerations. For this activity jot down a list of the kinds of people or activities you think *should not* be covered by a right of privacy/confidentiality.

Comment   You may feel that involvement in any of a wide range of criminal activities, such as child abuse, drug dealing, money laundering, terrorism, and so on should remove people's rights to privacy/confidentiality. We could summarise this position: 'there should be no right to keep private those activities which harm other people'. It was in this spirit that the government established a register of sexual offenders under the Sexual Offences Act 1997 (Home Office, 1996b) and supervision registers (in England) for people with mental illness diagnoses regarded as dangerous to others (Department of Health, 1995a).

The same formula could provide a justification for overriding an organisation's attempts to keep safety hazards or unsafe levels of staffing a secret by including 'gagging' clauses in the contracts of employees.

Some people also consider that a person should not have a right to privacy or confidentiality of information if this right means that harm will come to them. They would like to see a formula such as: 'there should be no right for a person to keep private those activities which will harm him or herself'.

As this activity suggests, codes of confidentiality usually have exclusions for people who have committed certain kinds of criminal offences and/or may be a danger to themselves and others. In fact, the law regarding confidentiality and privacy with regard to people who are merely a risk to themselves is extremely complicated and somewhat contradictory. In brief, the situation is that if an adult is put at risk by their own desire for confidentiality, then that is their affair. Only if they can be regarded as mentally incapacitated and hence unfit to make this decision can their rights to confidentiality be legally breached (Law Society/British Medical Association, 1995). Otherwise, you have no authority to intervene. This is the sort of situation that volunteers with the Samaritans (the telephone helpline for people who are desperate and suicidal) can encounter:

> *You do just have to listen, sometimes for hours while the person is dying of an overdose or bleeding to death at the end of the phone, and knowing that if you dialled 1471, you could probably trace the call, and alert the emergency services and save their life. But if the person doesn't want that then that's their right. That's how Sams do it.*

> *(Samaritan volunteer)*

In contrast to the Samaritans' approach, the operational policies of prisons and hospitals make it a requirement for staff to report on the suicidal intentions of inmates. All this is just an aspect of a more general legal confusion about how far people have the right to harm themselves intentionally, and how far others have an obligation to prevent them doing so.

Matters are rather clearer with regard to confidentiality and people who are engaged in criminal activity, or who might harm others. Many health and social care workers get to know information relevant to criminal offences, particularly those committed in a domestic context such as sexual or physical abuse, and information about illegal immigration, illicit drug use, benefit fraud, various kinds of 'under-age' offences: drinking, driving and sexual behaviour. Much of this information they discover under circumstances of confidentiality. There are no legal penalties for failing to report this information and in practice many practitioners do not volunteer such information to the police or immigration authorities, unless someone else's safety is at risk. However, in certain circumstances, the courts can override the usual confidentiality of medical or social work records - and can impose penalties if a practitioner refuses to breach confidentiality when required to do so by the courts.

As we noted in Section 3, people who work in health and social care are usually regarded by the civil courts as having a 'duty of confidentiality'. This makes it legal for employers to dismiss them for breaching confidentiality and allows service users to sue them (or their agencies) for damages if confidentiality is breached. However, the courts may also regard people who work in health and social care as having a duty to warn and a duty to protect (Rapaport, 1996) when the safety of a third party is involved. The case usually cited in this respect is the Tarasoff case (Stone, 1984). Here a psychotherapist, knowing that his client had an intention to kill someone, failed to disclose this. The killing took place and the psychotherapist was successfully sued by the victim's relatives. Thus the civil law lays contradictory duties on people who work in health and social care.

We have seen that most agencies and most professional groups have policies or codes of practice to aid them in making decisions in particular cases, and these differ. But a general consideration is always this question, 'Will more harm be done by maintaining confidentiality than by breaching it?'

This is often a question which is difficult to answer, partly because it involves predicting the future, and partly because giving a benefit to one person may be doing harm to another. Dilemmas of this kind can be especially acute where no criminal act has been committed, yet the client's behaviour constitutes a risk to someone else, and the information has been obtained in confidence.

4.2 Confidentiality, carers and relatives

In strictly legal terms the adult relatives, partners or friends of an adult service user seem rarely to have any more rights to receive service information about the service user than any other member of the public if the person concerned is capable of making decisions for him- or herself. Relatives and other co-residents only have the same rights as any other member of the public when their own safety is threatened by not disclosing the information to them. Where the service user is deemed incapable of making decisions, legally information may be shared with 'next of kin' or with a legal guardian on a need-to-know basis without consent, unless before becoming incapacitated the service user explicitly requested that this should not be done. In practice, although this is nowhere written down as policy, many services behave as if a client had given 'implicit consent' for some confidential matters to be shared with informal carers or other relatives, even to the extent of disclosing terminal diagnoses to relatives and not to the dying person (Benson and Britten, 1996)!

There are situations in which confidentiality from relatives becomes a very delicate matter indeed. For example, in cases of suspected child, spouse or elder abuse, the abused person, or some other witness, cannot be assured of confidentiality because if the suspicion is confirmed services cannot legally let the matter remain confidential. In the fields of drug abuse, mental health and learning disabilities, practitioners have, recently at least, tended to take a hard line in asserting the clients' right to prevent information about themselves being shared with relatives. This is in line with a belief that people with mental health problems and people with learning disabilities should have their autonomy as individuals upheld. Issues of confidentiality can then give rise to conflicts of interest between service users and informal carers. The former often want independence and privacy from their relatives, while the latter often feel that, although they shoulder the main burden of care, services keep them in the dark:

> *We take the bulk of the caring and the worry, we are the ones who cope in the night or who drive miles in the hope he will attend his programme ... We are, or feel, totally excluded from your updates on his condition.*
>
> *(Quoted in Shepherd* et al.*, 1994, p. 50)*

All the major research on the carers of people with mental health problems seems to show that carers feel information they need is kept confidential from them (Borthwick, 1993; Shepherd *et al.*, 1994).

Key point

- The aim to involve informal carers as partners in care may sometimes be challenged by the person cared for asserting their rights not to have confidential information disclosed to informal carers.

4.3 Disclosure in the public interest

There is sometimes a conflict between:

- the need to co-ordinate services
- the need to protect the public
- the need to protect the confidentiality of information
- the client's right to determine who shall see records about him or her.

This section considers this conflict by looking at a very well-known case which exemplifies the difficulties of co-ordinating care at the same time as keeping information confidential. This is the case of Christopher Clunis. What happened to him is similar in many respects to many of those other cases where someone with a mental illness diagnosis has killed someone and where this has been subject to an inquiry (Muijen, 1995). Such cases are rare (Royal College of Psychiatrists, 1996) but when they happen result in extensive news coverage and throw the health and social care agencies concerned into disarray.

Christopher Clunis killed Jonathon Zito, a man who was a complete stranger to him. In the inquiry which followed the death (Ritchie *et al.*, 1994) it emerged that Clunis had a long history of contacts with services, moving through various mental hospitals, moving on to and off the case load of various social services departments and between different hostels and supported accommodation. He was also 'known' to the police and had been on probation from time to time. What really marks the case is the way in which he was always getting separated from the records made about him. Thus he suddenly appeared as a 'new case' in a new agency and everything started from scratch, and then perhaps his records caught up with him or perhaps they did not. In these regards this case is a model of how not to co-ordinate community mental health care.

Inefficiencies on the part of various service agencies played an important part as did the inherent difficulties of transferring cases between agencies. But so also did Clunis's tendency to disappear, to refuse to give details about himself and, on one occasion, to change his name.

In addition, it also seems as if deference to Clunis's rights to confidentiality played a part in the tragedy. It didn't take long before whichever service was dealing with him learned that Clunis was liable to violent outbursts and to sexually harassing behaviour. However, there were at least 15 occasions when practitioners who knew this did not pass this information on to another agency which they knew he had contact with. Sometimes this was probably just sloppy practice. But according to witness statements sometimes this was due to the belief that if these facts were known about him he would be treated disadvantageously.

It may have been an important feature of the case that Clunis was black and that practitioners played down how dangerous he was in a misguided application of anti-discriminatory practice (see Unit 11). For example, it was for this reason that a psychiatric social worker said he did 'not want to stigmatise the patient, or label him in any way as violent or difficult' (Ritchie *et al.*, 1994, p. 37). In the opinion of Vernon Harris, who is a black equal opportunities trainer, this kind of under-reaction is just as racist as over-reaction:

'Large gaps' in care of man who killed, inquiry decides

Hospital error freed man for killing spree

Discharged schizophrenics: Attacks raise disturbing questions over social services' support for mentally ill in the community

Murder that followed a cycle of neglect

Psychiatric patient may sue health bodies for £500,000

'My wife was a schizophrenic, but the doctors let her out. They gave her a month's supply of tablets and told her to get on with it. So she went home and drowned my two beautiful sons'

Mental patient freed to kill

Schizophrenic killer given probation
Grandfather, 83, pushed over wall by man being cared for in the community

Social work staff admit errors over killer lodger

Review slams social services over death

Car was 'lethal weapon' for schizophrenic

Although killings by people with mental health problems, and deaths of children at the hands of their parents, are rare, they are very newsworthy. They blight the careers of practitioners and cause considerable disruption to services while inquiries proceed. Nearly all inquiries have found that poor record keeping is an important contributory factor in such disasters

If they see a black man, vicious and out of control, it is not a racist act to say so. Stereotyping is racist, when the example of one black person is used to classify black people as a group. People are individuals and they must be treated as such.

(Harris, 1994, in Thompson, 1995, p. 14)

And Ratna Dutt of the Race Equality Unit of the National Institute for Social Work says:

Over-reaction, under-reaction, or no reaction at all to black people with mental health problems is a major issue to us. Any of those positions are dangerous and discriminate against black people. If because of such misguided judgement a client ends up killing someone, that is not doing the client or society any favours.

(Quoted in Thompson, 1995, p. 14)

The truth about Clunis's dangerousness was especially kept from accommodation providers, and this is entirely understandable. Social workers and similar practitioners very often have to 'market' a service user to a provider of accommodation (and often to GPs too) and it is not surprising that they do so by withholding discrediting information on the grounds of 'client confidentiality'. The result was that Clunis came to hostels and other kinds of accommodation without the staff being forewarned of the risk he posed to them and other residents. Not long after this case a volunteer was killed in a hostel catering for people with mental health problems (Davies *et al.*, 1995).

It may or may not be the case that the unco-ordinated care experienced by Christopher Clunis led to the death of Jonathon Zito. But it was certainly the case that many hostel staff and residents were placed at considerable risk because information about him was withheld from them. So, as it turned out, were members of the public. Commenting on a number of similar cases, Kent (1996) identifies inadequate recording practice as one of a number of important common features.

Close scrutiny of records seems invariably to lead to serious questions about their accuracy, usefulness and accessibility to other relevant professionals. Incomplete care plans, inaccurate factual information and lost or missing records appear constantly in these inquiries.

(Kent, 1996, p. 18)

Key points

- Those who run services are frequently presented with dilemmas in trying to balance the right of individuals to have their affairs kept private with:

  – the need to share private information in order to co-ordinate services

  – the need to protect the interests and safety of others.

- There are elaborate doctrines concerning confidentiality and consent, but these are often difficult to apply to particular cases.

Conclusion

There were five core questions for this unit. The first of these was:

- **Why do we need records, and what functions do records and recording perform in health and social care organisations?**

Section 1 of the unit suggested seven different functions for recording. These are shown in Table 1. Although they are sometimes difficult to distinguish one from another, they were accountability, authorisation, decision making, monitoring, co-ordination, making practice systematic and learning from experience or making relationships. Different combinations of these functions require different kinds of records in terms of format, content and process of recording.

The second core question was:

- **What do the users of services need from records and how can recording best serve their needs?**

This question was also discussed in Section 1. There, we suggested that what service users and informal carers need from records is information stating who is accountable for providing care, in what ways and how they can complain if this is not done. They need a record of their rights, their entitlements, and what other people are authorised to do to them. And they need to have access to adequate information – in a usable form – so that they can make their own decisions about health and social care, and be able to give consent which is informed. Also, where records show who has promised to do what, service users will know who to get in touch with if the co-ordination of care breaks down.

We saw that records best meet service users' needs when they are clear, accessible, accurate and fit for purpose. They are also most helpful when they include the information that service users think is important to them. One way of achieving this is to involve service users and carers in recording information about themselves. Section 1 discussed ways in which people can have a role in compiling their own records and some of the difficulties that can arise in the process.

The third core question was:

- **Who controls information and the way it is shared?**

The best way in which users of services can control information about them is by not providing it in the first place. But, as Section 2 noted, they often don't have much choice about this. Some kinds of information have to be provided under the duress of the criminal justice system or the immigration service. But most services require some information to be provided, simply as a condition of service. In fact, the doctrine of implicit consent is often so 'implicit' that service users don't know about it.

So it seems that the answer to the third question is that service-providing organisations and professionals generally control information (although, as noted above, some service users do have a key role in the construction of their own records). Apart from refusing to provide information there is little service users can do to control the way information about them is shared. In this respect they have to rely on the people who work in health and social care services to tell them what their rights are under whichever confidentiality policy is relevant at the time. And they have to trust workers to treat information about them confidentially. Professionals do not have it all their own way though, as they operate within legal and policy constraints and service users have increasingly clear rights of access to any material about them under the terms of the Data Protection Act 1998 and the Freedom of Information Act 2000.

Section 3 outlined some of the devices used in attempts to enforce confidentiality on workers in health and care and addressed the fourth core question:

- **What is a duty of confidentiality and how does a confidentiality policy work?**

To get some understanding of both policy and practice in relation to confidentiality, we looked at the procedures in operation in one fictitious agency, NIAS, and the practical and ethical issues that occur when you try to apply such a policy.

This led to the last of the core questions:

- **How can a balance be struck between respecting the privacy of one individual by keeping recorded information confidential, and protecting the interests of others who may have a legitimate need to know this information?**

The short answer to this question is, 'often with great difficulty'. As in many aspects of health and social care benefits to one individual may well be achieved to the disadvantage of another (Kohner, 1996). But the fact that it is difficult to strike the right balance does not remove the need to make decisions in cases such as the ones discussed in Section 4. So a longer answer to the question posed above would need to address the different elements that contribute to effective decision making in specific cases. These include: explicit confidentiality policies, the legal framework governing the situation (i.e. do you have a choice about disclosure?), training in the application of confidentiality procedures, making sure that individuals know about and have access to complaints processes, and monitoring/supervision.

Records are such a ubiquitous aspect of care that you have not finished with them yet. The next unit in this block is about accountability. As you have already seen, what is on the record makes people accountable for what they have or have not done. This includes whether they have made the records they are supposed to make, and whether they have consulted the records they are supposed to consult. So material on records will also be an important feature of the next unit.

References

Audit Commission (1995a) *Setting the Records Straight*, TSO, London.

Audit Commission (1995b) *For Your Information: A Study of Management Information Systems in the Acute Hospital*, TSO, London.

Benson, T. (1997) 'The message is the medium', Health Service Journal, 30 January, pp. 4–5.

Benson, J. and Britten, N. (1996) 'Respecting the autonomy of cancer patients when talking with their families: qualitative analysis of semi-structured interviews', British Medical Journal, Vol. 313, pp. 729–31.

Borthwick, A. (1993) *Invisible Pain: The Experience of Being a Relative of a Person with Schizophrenia*, National Schizophrenia Fellowship Scotland, Edinburgh.

Brownlie, I. (ed.) (1983) *Basic Documents on Human Rights* (2 edn), Clarendon, Oxford.

CCETSW/City and Guilds of London Institute (1997) *Draft Revision Standards: Care Level 3*, Joint Awarding Bodies (CCETSW and City and Guilds), London.

Cross, M. (1997a) 'For the record', Health Services Journal, 30 January, pp. 7–8.

Davies, N., Lingham, R., Prior, C. and Sims, A. (1995) *Report of the Inquiry into the Circumstances Leading to the Death of Jonathon Newby (a volunteer worker) on 9th October 1993 in Oxford*, Oxfordshire Health Authority, Oxford.

Department of Health (1991a) *Care Management and Assessment: Practitioners' Guide*, TSO, London.

Department of Health (1994a) *Inspection of Assessment and Care Management in Social Services Departments October 1993–March 1994*, TSO, London.

Department of Health (1995a) *Building Bridges: Guide to Arrangements for Inter-agency Working for the Care and Protection of Severely Mentally Ill People*, TSO, London.

Department of Health (1995c) *Acting on Complaints*, Department of Health, London.

Department of Health (1996a) *The Protection and Use of Patient Information: Guidance from the Department of Health*, Department of Health, London.

Department of Health (1996c) *Coordinating Community Mental Health Care: The Care Programme Approach*, Open University/Department of Health Social Services Inspectorate, Milton Keynes.

Dobson, R. (1996) 'Clients reject means tests', *Community Care*, 25–31 January, p. 9.

Downey, R. (1995) 'Survey reveals effect of community care on staff', *Community Care*, 30 March–5 April, p. 3.

Feldbaum, E. and Dick, R. (1997) *Electronic Patient Records, Smart Cards and Confidentiality*, Financial Times Pharmaceuticals and Healthcare Publishing, London.

General Medical Council (1993) *Professional Conduct and Discipline: Fitness to Practise*, General Medical Council, London.

Gilhooly, L. and McGhee, S. (1991) 'Medical records: practicalities and principles of patient possession', *Journal of Medical Ethics*, Vol. 17, pp. 138–43.

Gomm, R. (1989) *Counselling in the Renal Unit*, unpublished paper.

Harris, V. (1994) *Review of 'The Care and Treatment of Christopher Clunis': A Black Perspective*, Race Equality Unit, National Institute for Social Work, London.

Hogg, C. (1994) *Beyond the Patient's Charter: A practical guide for people working in the health service*, Health Rights, London.

Home Office (1996b) *protecting the public*, TSO, London.

Kent, I. (1996) 'Reporting back', *Community Care*, 22–28 February, pp. 18–19.

Kohner, N. (1996) *The Moral Maze of Practice: A Stimulus for Reflection and Discussion*, King's Fund, London.

Law Society/British Medical Association (1995) *Assessment of Mental Capacity: Guidance for Doctors and Lawyers*, British Medical Association, London.

Lindsey, M. and Russell, D. (1999) *Once-a-day one or more people with learning disabilities are likely to be in contact with your primary healthcare team. How can you help them?*, Department of Health, London.

Muijen, M. (1995) 'Scare in the community: Part five: care of mentally ill people', *Community Care*, 7–13 September, supplement pp. i–viii.

National Health Service Executive (1995) *Handling Confidential Information in Contracting: A Code of Practice*, NHSE, Leeds.

National Health Service Executive (1996a) Complaints. *Listening. Acting. Improving: Guidance on Implementation of the NHS Complaints Procedures*, Department of Health, Leeds.

National Health Service Executive (1996b) *Promoting Clinical Effectiveness*, Department of Health, Leeds.

National Health Service Training Directorate (1995) *Just for the Record: A Guide to Record Keeping for Health Care Professionals*, NHSTD, Bristol.

Northern Ireland Office (1991) *Care Management: Guide on Assessment and the Provision of Community Care*, Northern Ireland Office, Belfast.

Nursing and Midwifery Council (2002) *Code of Professional Conduct*, NMC, London.

Powell, T. (1992) *The Mental Health Handbook*, Winslow Press, Bicester.

Rapaport, J. (1996) *'Confidentiality and mental health care'*, Practice Nursing, Vol. 7, No. 6, pp. 12–14.

Ritchie, J., Dick, D. and Lingham, R. (1994) *The Report of the Inquiry into the Care and Treatment of Christopher Clunis*, TSO, London.

Royal College of Psychiatrists (1996) *Report of the Confidential Inquiry into Homicides and Suicides by Mentally Ill People (Boyd report)*, Royal College of Psychiatrists for the Confidential Inquiry into Homicides and Suicides by Mentally Ill People, London.

Shepherd, G., Murray, A. and Muijen, M. (1994) *Relative Values: Differing Views of Users, Family Carers and Professionals on Services for People with Schizophrenia in the Community*, Sainsbury Centre for Mental Health, London.

Silicon Bridge Research (1997) *The EPR Report*, Silicon Bridge Research, London.

Stone, A. (1984) *Law, Psychiatry and Morality*, American Psychiatry Press, New York.

Thompson, A. (1995) 'Tablets of stone', *Community Care*, 12–18 October, pp. 14–15.

Valios, N. (1996) 'Assessment queries "offensive" says client', *Community Care*, 2–8 May, p. 9.

Villeneau, L. (1994) *'Confidentiality', in Mindfile 3: Practice Guidelines*, MIND, London.

Waller, T. (1993) *Drugswork 5: Working with GPs*, Institute for Study of Drug Dependence, London.

Walshe, K. and Ham, C. (1997) 'Who's acting on the evidence?', *Health Services Journal*, 3 April, pp. 22–5.

Watson, J. and Taylor, R. (1996) 'Standard Practice', *Community Care*, 8–14 February, pp. 28–9.

http://www.doh.gov.uk/dpa98/ The Data Protection Act 1998: Protection and Use of Patient Information.

Acknowledgements

Grateful acknowledgement is made to the following sources for permission to reproduce material in this unit:

Table

Table 2: Hogg, C. (1994) *Beyond the Patient's Charter: A Practical Guide for People Working in the Health Service*, Health Rights Ltd.

Illustrations

p. 47: Courtesy of Link 51 Storage Products Ltd; *p. 59*: Courtesy of Peter Cochrane; *p. 62*: Powell, T. (1992) *Mental Health Handbook*, Winslow Press, by permission of Trevor Powell.

Unit 24
Accountability

Originally prepared for the course team by Roger Gomm

Revised by Marion Reichart and Danielle Turney

While you are working on Unit 24, you will need:

- Course Reader
- Offprints Book
- Care Systems and Structures
- Wallchart

Contents

Introduction

One of the five K100 principles of good practice is to ensure that people receive appropriate services. But how *can* this be ensured? In this unit we explore what it means to be accountable, who is accountable and to whom they are accountable. To be accountable means that a person or an agency can be judged as to whether they have done *what* should have been done and in the *way* it should have been done. How, for example, is Dr. Li, whom you met in Unit 22 as a GP at the Grove Health Centre, held to account for how effectively she diagnoses and treats patients, how the surgery is run and how records are kept, as well as how effectively people are informed about the services of the Health Centre?

Signs like this on the back of lorries appear to make drivers accountable for the quality of their driving. But a sign alone does not make 'accountability' happen. What counts as 'bad driving' may vary depending on who is behind the lorry; for example, a cyclist may have a different view of 'bad driving' to a car driver. Deciding on bad driving may depend on the type of road, for example whether it is a motorway or a narrow country lane, or on the time of day or the weather conditions. It could vary from observer to observer depending on their personality. And if you decided that you were observing bad driving, at what point would you do something about it? Would you note the telephone number down? If so, when would you phone to complain? This example shows that accountability may not be quite as straightforward as it first appears. But despite that, it seems to be a word on everyone's lips in health and social care contexts. So in this unit, we will be considering why that should be.

Section 1 of this unit looks at the ways in which people can be 'held to account', and what that means. It goes on to consider one particular aspect: accountability to the public, who claim a right to see that public money is being spent for purposes of which they approve. It addresses the questions 'accountability for what?' and 'accountable to whom?'

Section 2 examines why it is that during the past twenty years the accountability of practitioners and agencies in health and social care has become such an important issue.

Section 3 considers what it is like to be accountable. It looks at a case study of a residential care worker dismissed from his job. This case study illustrates how difficult it sometimes is to decide whether an organisation or an individual is to blame when something goes wrong. The accountability of practitioners and professionals is then considered by examining the experiences of nurses who feel that they are accountable for matters over which they have no control. The question here is 'who is accountable and to whom?'

Section 4 looks at how people who work in health and social care respond to being accountable. Sometimes they do this through adopting tactics which are called 'defensive practice' and which undermine attempts to make them accountable. The section examines the conditions under which practitioners find accountability acceptable, and how appropriate structures of accountability might promote good quality care.

Core questions

- What does it mean to be accountable?

- Why has there been pressure to increase the level of accountability in health and social care?

- What problems arise for people and agencies who are made accountable and how do they respond to these?

Section 1
What is accountability?

Being accountable means that you have an obligation to describe and justify your actions to others so that they can judge whether you have fulfilled your duties adequately. It also implies that if you have not you will be held responsible. So, in effect, accountability means that the activities of a person or agency are subject to a degree of control by others.

Accountability is a key feature of the work of many professionals, for example, nurses, police officers, social workers, doctors and teachers. These are people working in public services; they are responsible for decisions about people's lives and often have power and influence over them. Abuse of power and malpractice can lead to a sharp decline in trust.

Key points

- Being accountable means having an obligation to describe and justify actions, so that others can judge whether duties have been fulfilled adequately.

- It implies that something important (and perhaps something negative) will happen because the judgement has been made.

1.1 Directions of accountability

'Accountable to whom?' is always an important issue. There are a large number of directions in which someone or some agency might be accountable, often at the same time.

Here are some directions of accountability, which often apply to health and social care practitioners and agencies.

- **Public accountability.** 'The public' is a large and diverse group, so effective public accountability usually involves nominating or appointing people to represent the 'public interest'. For example, a management committee oversees the activities of NIAS (although day-to-day management of the service is carried out by the manager they have approved). The members of the management committee are elected at an annual general meeting which anyone may attend, so any member of the public can put themselves forward for election. The AGM is also the place where the management committee will have to give a 'public account' of their activities over the previous year.

- **Legal accountability.** This means accountability to the courts and to other judicial bodies such as tribunals - for example, the tribunals which arbitrate disputes about welfare benefits or the tribunals to which people detained under mental health legislation can appeal against their detention (Department of Health, 1996). Disputes about whether some agency has fulfilled its obligations can end up in the courts. The criminal law makes everyone accountable and crimes committed in the course of health or social care work are still crimes.

- **Accountability to regulators and inspectors**. In Unit 23 we came across Eventide, where Mr Thomas Li stayed when he needed respite care. A registered home of this kind will be open to inspection by a number of agencies. For example, nursing and residential homes are accountable to the independent inspectorates of the health authority and the social services (or social work) authority respectively, although often these operate as a single, joint inspectorate. You considered this form of regulation in Unit 8. Eventide will also be inspected by the fire safety authority and will need to meet other standards enforceable by the environmental health department and local authority. And in the event of a complaint about discrimination, the Commission for Racial Equality, Equal Opportunities Commission and the Disability Rights Commission could be involved. Other important regulators and inspectorates in health and social care are listed in Section 3 'Regulation and Inspection' of Care Systems and Structures.

- **Accountability to central government**. The government issues guidance and sets performance targets for most public agencies. The agencies have to provide information so that they can be judged in terms of whether they are following the guidance or meeting the targets. For example, in 2003, one of the key aims in the NHS is to reduce waiting lists. Performance targets have been set and hospitals have to gather information to show whether or not they have reduced waiting lists sufficiently.

- **Accountability as an employee or employer**. A contract of employment makes an employee of a health or care agency accountable for doing whatever their contract specifies, and this is usually spelt out in greater detail in job descriptions and operational policies. Often what employees have to do is determined by the law, by central government guidance, by purchaser/provider contracts or by central government performance targets. Contracts of employment also make employers accountable to employees. Employers, for example, are responsible for equal opportunities, and the health and safety of people working for them. They have a duty of care towards employees.

- **Accountability as a professional**. Some health and social care workers are subject to regulatory bodies which maintain registers from which practitioners can be removed: for example, doctors (General Medical Council), nurses (The Nursing and Midwifery Council) and the professions allied to medicine, such as chiropodists, physiotherapists or occupational therapists (Council for the Professions Supplementary to Medicine). In the social care field, the General Social Care Council will maintain a register of social workers, care workers and such like. Professionals who are registered in this way are bound to follow their profession's codes of conduct and may be 'struck off' (that is, deregistered) if they don't. Complaints can also be made about professionals to their professional body.

- **Accountability to service users through complaints procedures**. Complaints procedures allow aggrieved service users to bring individual practitioners or agencies to account. When local complaints procedures fail, service users may take their case to the commissioners or ombudsmen for local government (local 'administration'), for the health service, or for Parliament. Section 3 of Care Systems and Structures gives further details. Alternatively, when complaints procedures fail, a case may go to the courts. In the case of professional workers, complaints may also be made to their professional body.

- **Accountability to service users**. Accountability to service users may derive from what is promised to them in a care plan, like the one for Arthur Durrant we looked at in Unit 23, or what promises practitioners make verbally. Practitioners such as Beverley Jackson and Pat Walsh are accountable to service users in their daily interactions with them. When arranging appointments or follow-up for patients at the Grove Health Centre, Pat Walsh is providing a service which makes her accountable directly to patients.

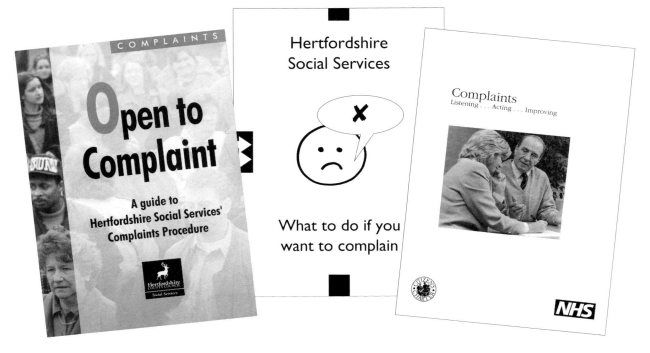

If services are to be accountable to service users, service users first need to know what they have a right to expect – written care plans help here – and then need to know how to complain when they don't get it. Complaints procedures became much more accessible during the 1990s

As you can see, people who work in health and social care may be accountable in numerous different ways, sometimes as individuals, and sometimes because the agency they work for is made accountable. There are very few situations in which only one kind of accountability applies. Indeed, it was very difficult to write a logical list, because the different forms of accountability often turn into one another.

1.2 Accountability structures

Accountability sounds fine as a principle, but it does not amount to much unless there are accountability structures in place. You have come across a number of cases in Block 5 (such as Ruth and Adam) where there was no proper mechanism for making this known.

Any accountability structure will have some of the features shown in the box below.

The main features of accountability structures

- There will be *explicit statements about responsibilities*. Beverley Jackson, who works for *Care Matters*, would have a contract of employment stating the number of hours she is to work and the kind of duties she has to carry out. Further details may be provided in the form of a care plan for individual clients, which states what tasks are expected of her during her visits.

- There will be *procedures for making performance or outcomes observable*. On completing a home visit, Beverley Jackson might be asked to fill out a time sheet and have this signed by the client. She may be required to record tasks carried out or produce a weekly 'progress sheet' to show to her team leader.

- There are likely to be *penalties and sanctions* against inadequate performance and there may also be rewards for excellent performance. Positive client feedback, for instance, may assist Beverley in gaining a higher rate of pay.

- There will be *mechanisms for bringing a person or organisation to account*. These might include a complaints procedure through which clients can bring Beverley to account. Weekly meetings with her team leader offer the opportunity to discuss her workload and reflect on what went well and what could be improved. Beverly might like to raise questions or request training in a particular area. The employing agency, *Care Matters*, is accountable to her as an employer and is under a duty of care towards her. Conversely, Beverley also has obligations and appraisal or supervision meetings, or annual reports on performance are mechanisms for bringing her to account.

- To protect people against unjust accusations, there are likely to be *formal procedures for investigating alleged shortcomings*. Examples include disciplinary hearings, grievance procedures, committees of inquiry, the procedures of the civil and criminal law, and various systems of appeal from one decision-making body to another.

Activity 1   **Your experience of accountability**

Allow about 15 minutes   The purpose of this activity is for you to relate the main features of accountability structures to your own experiences. Instead of Beverley, think about your own circumstance. Select a situation where you are, or have been, the person who is accountable. Choose a health or welfare context, if you can. But if this is not possible, an example involving education, or housing, or as a provider or user of services, or as an employee in an office or factory will be fine. When you have chosen your example, think about which features of accountability structures applied to you.

- Explicit statements about responsibilities
- Procedures for making performances/outcomes observable
- Penalties/sanctions
- Mechanisms for bringing to account
- Formal procedures for investigating allegations

Can you see gaps in the accountability structures applying to you? If so, what consequences could arise? There is no comment following this activity, but **keep your notes** because you will use them again later.

1.3 Trust and accountability

Are all these structures necessary and is all this energy and expense justified? Would it not be better just to *trust* people to do what they should? At what point do we need to move beyond trust to formal structures of accountability?

Activity 2   **From mutual trust to formal accountability**

Allow about 15 minutes   For this activity find Offprint 31, 'Empowering empowerment: professionals and self-advocacy projects', by Jan Wallcraft. The story she tells is of a project which was transformed into something very different from what the originators wanted. It moved from one in which everything could be done by informal mutual agreement among people who trusted each other, into one in which accountability was put on a formal basis. Read the article and jot down your ideas about:

(a)   whether this transformation was inevitable or avoidable

(b)   whether it was justifiable.

Comment   (a)   This transformation was almost inevitable once the group received funding from a public source. Public funding nearly always brings a measure of accountability for how the money is spent. It was also inevitable once the group became responsible for the welfare of more than its founder members: responsible as employers and as providers of a service to others. In providing finance to such organisations, social services authorities and health authorities are extending their own 'duty of care', for which they are accountable.

(b)   There is a good case for saying that it would have been unjustifiable to have funded this group from public sources and to have allowed it to go on operating in the original unaccountable way, even though this blighted the dream of the original group.

The original self-advocacy group was a collection of people who were in agreement with each other. As a group they had some responsibilities for each other, but none for anyone else. This was the kind of organisation in which people could reach agreements informally and trust each other to carry out what they had promised to do. Failing that, if there were disagreements and broken promises these could be settled by aggrieved people leaving the group. Indeed, if the group had collapsed, then only those who were members would have been affected. So long as they agreed with each other there was no great need for rules or constitutions, written job descriptions or much else to put the accountability of members on a more formal footing. Nonetheless, it is wise for even the most informal groups to have some ground rules in terms of which disagreements can be resolved (The Open University, 1992).

However, this situation changed when the group received funding from a public source in order to supply a public service. Then they were required to do proper budgeting, keep proper accounts and submit them to audit, to draw up and keep to the kinds of rules about employees that employers are supposed to abide by, and make themselves accountable to the Inland Revenue for the payment of PAYE taxation. The article does mention that the group had to draw up and follow a written constitution and among other things this would define the proper procedures for making decisions. Through the minutes of its meetings, then, the group became accountable for showing that decisions were made correctly according to the constitution and not on the whim or fancy of someone who just felt like making any old decision. Accountability to 'the public' may be achieved by having a public annual general meeting at which its accounts would be displayed and a report of its work given.

Key points

- When public money is dispensed it is usually accompanied by an obligation to account for how it is spent.
- When the statutory health or social care services issue contracts to providers, they remain accountable for the welfare of the people who use the services.

1.4 Public accountability and performance indicators

Most people would agree with the general principle that if services are funded with public money, they should be made publicly accountable for (a) how the money is spent, and (b) their performance. An increasingly common way of attempting to do this, across public services as a whole, is for central government to set up performance targets or indicators and to require public services to provide information on whether, or how far, they are meeting them.

The 'league tables' of educational performance which are published about the achievements of individual schools and educational authorities constitute some of the most newsworthy performance indicators of all. But there are also performance indicators and targets for health authorities and local authorities including social services and social work agencies, housing, environmental health, probation and the police (Audit Commission, 1995). In June 2002, the first 'star ratings', ranging from zero to three stars, for services offered through local social services were awarded to London boroughs.

Making performance indicators work is not straightforward. There may be disagreement over what aspect of performance is to be monitored, how it is to be measured and how it can be achieved. Performance indicators are criticised for creating 'perverse incentives'. The concern is that in an effort to meet performance targets, such as shorter waiting lists, the quality of care will suffer. For example, the NHS efficiency index is criticised for encouraging NHS trusts to prioritise quantity and cost over quality (National Association of Health Authorities and Trusts, 1997). In '*A Question of Trust – Called to Account*', one of the Reith Lectures on the BBC, Professor O'Neill (2002) observed that performance indicators have a deep effect on professional and institutional behaviour:

'If waiting lists can be reduced faster by concentrating on certain medical procedures hospitals have reason so to do even if medical priorities differ. Perverse incentives are real incentives.'

Professor Onora O'Neill (The Reith Lectures, BBC Radio 4, 2002)

Another concern is that performance indicators are not telling the whole story. They are seen to lead to simplistic judgements about the performance of different agencies without fully taking their particular circumstances into consideration (Combes, 1995).

A further difficulty with performance indicators is that they need to describe adequate and inadequate performance in detail and in a way that can be precisely measured. Added difficulties have been created by ever changing definitions and targets to be measured and by having to keep up with the volume of new guidance regulations, rules and procedures, for example from the Department of Health (www.doh.gov.uk). Whatever the difficulties, though, it appears that performance indicators and targets are here to stay.

Ordinary people, actual or potential service users and members of the public are increasingly sought out to be involved in setting standards and monitoring performance. One mechanism by which a greater degree of 'working in partnership' can be achieved is through citizen juries or focus groups, as we discussed in Unit 22.

The use of 'citizens' juries' (or 'focus groups') to inform the planning of health and social care suggests that 'ordinary people' can quite quickly develop the expertise necessary if they are provided with the relevant information in a form they can understand. Citizens' juries developed first in Germany and the USA and are increasingly being used in Britain to tap public opinion with regard to setting priorities for health care purchasing. The following extract gives you a glimpse of what citizen jurors learn from the process, and what helps them to come to informed decisions.

Open court

A citizens' jury on drug use proved an education for its participants and changed their view of how to tackle the problem. Joy Ogden reports.

Last week David Goldring's instincts were to 'go ballistic' with drug users. Police should take a tough line, clinics were too soft an option, drugs were a real danger. But that was last week.

This week he is not so sure. Four days on a citizens' jury set him thinking and now he believes – with almost evangelical fervour – that other people should be educated about drugs as he has been so that they too can come to an informed opinion. Most of his fellow jurors feel the same.

The way the jury heard the ex-pert evidence and – in the light of what its members were told – changed their views carries important lessons for health authorities faced with difficult consultation processes on highly charged and complex issues.

Mr Goldring is a 33-year-old Afro-Caribbean finance officer, and was one of 16 jurors chosen at random to mirror the population of the south London borough of Lewisham.

[...]

Over four days at the end of April the jury heard testimonies from addicts, former addicts and recreational drug users. They weighed the evidence and cross-examined an impressive procession of expert witnesses from the health, education and police services ...

Lewisham council's policy officers, Brigitte Gohdes and Stella Clarke, took notes, then provided printed witness statements and summaries of issues raised at each day's debates, so jurors did not become overwhelmed by the volume of data. And there was a lot of information – sometimes conflicting – to process.

(Ogden, 1996, p. 12)

The extract you have just read relates to a scheme run by the Local Government Management Board covering seven local authorities and their associated health authorities. It was called 'The Democracy Project', and was experimenting with different forms of local consultation. At the same time the King's Fund Institute was running three pilot projects in three different health authorities (*King's Fund News*, Summer 1997, pp. 1–6). Three problems were mentioned earlier with regard to effective public involvement. Properly managed, the process of citizen jury deliberations seems to deal with the issue of *expertise* (see also Brochie and Wann, 1993). In the end, David and his fellow jurors decided that spending money on prescribing methadone for drug addicts was a worthwhile use of health service money. As for *motivation*, just how many people would be prepared to spend four days sitting on a citizens' jury is an open question. The £50 payment made in Lewisham probably helped, but there has been a long-term decline in public participation in public affairs. Citizens' juries are not *representative* in the democratic sense of the term, which implies being elected by a constituency to represent them. But if, like court juries, they are selected at random, then they are more likely to be representative in the statistical sense of the term; that is, representing the range of different types of people in an area.

The issue of public accountability is about how public affairs should be organised in general, and how public decisions should be made and their effects evaluated. This is especially difficult when there are many different groups with many different and conflicting interests (Cooper *et al.*, 1995). *Public accountability* is a different matter from accountability to people who use services.

Key points

- Publicly funded services imply public accountability – which is not the same as accountability to the people who use the services.

- Public accountability for health and social care services is an untidy matter, involving elements of electoral democracy (through elected local authorities), mechanisms of public involvement (through community care planning and locality commissioning), the publication of data in terms of performance indicators, and monitoring, inspection and regulation through bodies supposedly representing the public interest.

Section 2

Increasing accountability in health and social care

There is no doubt that from the end of the 1980s onwards those who work in health and social care have been subjected to increased accountability. Two significant trends which led to this increase were consumerism and managerialism.

2.1 Consumerism

The 1990s saw the development of very assertive consumer movements among those who use health and social care services. You read about one aspect of this – the self-advocacy movement – in Unit 22. This is only part of a wider trend which includes much more vigorous campaigning by the pressure groups representing the interests of service users: for example Mencap, Age Concern, ENABLE or the Alzheimers Society (McKechnie, 1996b). Their memberships go much further than the service users themselves, including carers, practitioners, academics, interested members of the public, and celebrities such as the late Princess Diana. Each group tries to make the headlines at least once a year when it publishes its annual report, and often more frequently, and the larger groups are well represented in Parliament by sympathetic MPs or members of the House of Lords.

Action by individual service users, whether supported by such groups or not, must also be added to the story. So, for example, in the NHS the number of complaints doubled between 1991 and 1995, and by 1994 it was paying out around £125 million per year in court and out-of-court settlements for costs and damages following lawsuits from patients and their relatives. Again, this is about double the bill for 1991 (Harris, 1996, p. 4). There is little evidence that the quality of care in the NHS was twice as bad in 1995 as in 1991, and the general opinion is that this increase in complaints and lawsuits reflects a greater willingness by consumers to bring health services to account. Social services have also seen an increase in complaints and litigation (Department of Health Social Services Inspectorate, 1994), and particularly in the use of judicial review by the courts, which was something hardly ever used before the mid-1980s. The following box tells you something about judicial reviews and gives an example.

Judicial reviews

Judicial reviews are High Court hearings to establish whether an authority such as a health authority, board or trust, a government department or, as in the example below, a social services or social work authority has acted according to the law, and/or according to procedures it has committed itself to. They are used particularly to clarify what the law is when there is some doubt about this. Thus the findings of judicial reviews make law for the future (Public Law Project, 1994; Gordon, 1993, pp. 55–65). For example, the way the Carers (Recognition and Services) Act 1995 was drafted left it unclear whether children who were informal carers were included and were entitled to an assessment of their needs as carers, or whether their entitlement to assessment as children in need under the Children Act 1989 excluded them from this. Newham Council interpreted the Carers Act to exclude young carers, and that left a 14-year-old, partially deaf girl having to wash her disabled sister in a washing-up bowl because the council refused to install a shower to assist with 'caring'. The judicial review was initiated by the child's mother and the 14-year-old, supported by the Carers National Association. The review found against Newham Council, which was ordered to install the shower and provide 17 days' respite care per year for the family. But the important outcome was that the case established that the needs of 'young carers' did fall under the Carers Act. In fact, Newham could, and probably should, have provided exactly the same under Section 17 of the Children Act: the shower to meet the needs of the younger sister, and respite care to meet the needs of the 14-year-old. These were their needs as children in both cases (Brindle, 1997).

The term 'consumer' was used advisedly above, because suing for redress is exactly what *consumers* do. It was part of Conservative government (1979–97) policy to encourage people to think of themselves as consumers of health and social care services. The national consumer organisations extended their interests from the commercial marketplace to the public health and care services, so there are now *Which?* reports on health and social care topics and similar reports from the Scottish Consumer Council (Scottish Consumer Council and Scottish Association of Health Councils, 1992). Some health and care pressure groups remodelled themselves on consumer organisations dealing with commercial products. The extract opposite shows you one of these in the form of the recruitment advertisement for the Patients Association, a consumer organisation for the patients of the NHS. It publishes a newspaper featuring patient complaints and advice about complaining, a very clear guide on how to make complaints (Hogg, 1996), and supports patients and relatives in making them.

Various aspects of government policy have clarified what service users have a right to expect from services. If you look back to the box on accountability structures in Section 1.2 you will see that the first item listed refers to statements about responsibilities. By clarifying what it is that service users have a right to expect, central government policy has automatically increased the accountability of services.

The fourth item listed for an accountability structure is about mechanisms for bringing individuals and agencies to account. Governments have required both health and social services to make their complaints procedures easier to understand and more easily available to service users. The inclusion of a complaints procedure is a usual condition attached to a contract with health or social services, and there can be few publicly funded voluntary sector agencies today which do not have service user charters or something similar. This is often as a result of a requirement imposed upon them by the statutory agency with which they have a contract or service level agreement. On the whole, most voluntary sector organisations have welcomed this (Kumar, 1997).

The reforms associated with the NHS and Community Care Act 1990 and its Northern Ireland equivalent also fostered the development of assertive consumerism among service users. This was particularly so with regard to community care planning. The requirement that these activities should be done through public consultation gave organised groups of service users the opportunity to question and influence the planning of services. In addition, the contracting out of care services to voluntary sector agencies, first, forced those agencies to be more accountable to those who provide their funds, as you glimpsed in the self-advocacy group example from Jan Wallcraft. And, second, it gave social and health services purchasers the opportunity to force voluntary sector agencies to make themselves more accountable to those who use their services.

Your Patients Association – We are here to listen CALL US WITH YOUR STORIES

We are here to make a difference for patients. We are here to listen, and then to respond. We are here to press for kinder, more access-ible, more suitable, services which deliver better health outcomes for millions of individual people. What works for you is our focus. And you tell us that what you want is for health workers to ask you about the 'quality of life' issues that matter to you before you agree to treatment. We agree.

The PA seeks *to listen* to what people want to tell us. Our 'Patient-line' is the most essential part of all our work. You can call us for advice on [0181 423 8999].

• We offer support, guidance, contacts

• We answer queries, and help people find answers which will work for them.

• The PA puts your views to policy makers, to politicians and to government – we make views heard where it counts.

• We seek to make desired changes actually happen, by exercising influence and by work-ing with managers – who want better services, and many of whose Health Authorities and NHS Trusts are members of the PA.

• The PA campaigns for change, and publicises your views widely in the media. We are called upon daily by the media for auth-oritative guidance and comment.

• We are consulted at many levels, because we have a distinc-tive voice.

• The PA is open to all. It speaks up for necessary change, based on the evidence, experi-ences, stories and knowledge patients share with us.

It is evidence that we need to be able to call upon. By analysing what patients tell us we can in-crease our authority and influ-ence. For this is indeed unique knowledge. Patients' stories of what happened to them must be applied to improving services.

(*Patients' Voices*, No. 1, Autumn 1996, p.1)

Thus the development of assertive consumerism and the 1990s reforms of health and social services developed together to make health and care agencies, and the individuals who work in them, more accountable to those who use the services. They may not be accountable enough in some people's view, and it might be argued that they are not accountable to the right people in the right ways, but they are much more accountable than they were before the 1990s.

2.2 Managerialism

At the same time that accountability to service users has increased, people who work in health and social care services have been made more accountable to their managers. Meanwhile, agencies themselves have been made more accountable:

• to central government directly, or

• to regulatory bodies which carry out government policy, or

• to inspecting bodies which investigate whether government policy is being implemented.

All of this puts pressure on the managers of health and social care services to direct the work of front-line workers more closely and make them more accountable for showing that they are actually following the procedures managers have laid down. This is one of the reasons for the large increase in record making discussed in Unit 23.

Management enthusiasm for this in the NHS is often enhanced by managers being paid on a performance-related basis, or having contracts which will not be renewed unless they meet specified performance targets.

2.3 Recent developments

After the Conservatives left office in 1997 New Labour kept up the pressure for greater accountability through its drive to 'modernise' public services (discussed more fully in Unit 27). The key words were 'targets' and 'standards'. Service providers seeking increased resources to improve the quality of their services, found that funding came with strings attached. They were set targets and were required to demonstrate that they had met them to specified standards. Thus we see ever more stringent requirements for monitoring and reviewing services. At the same time, there is pressure to increase the involvement of service users in planning and reviewing services, implying extended processes of accountability.

And has all this pressure to increase accountability actually improved the quality of services? It is very hard to say. People continue to complain about the services and want their complaints investigated. Ironically, accountability breeds accountability. The more people know about what happens in services, the more questions they ask and the more information they demand. Hardly a week seems to go by without some demand for more precisely defined standards, more monitoring or more regulation.

Key Points

- Health, social and other public services were all made more accountable during the 1990s. Two main, linked trends account for this:

  - the growth of an assertive consumer movement among those who used health and social care services (facilitated greatly by the NHS and Community Care Act 1990 and its Northern Ireland equivalent) provides opportunities for more public and service user involvement.

  - the development of a 'new managerialism' which made services much more accountable to central government, and thereby increased the power of service managers over professionals and other staff.

- The 'contract culture' has had a similar effect, making voluntary and private sector providers more accountable to the managers in the agencies which purchase services from them.

- Following the 1997 arrival of New Labour, the emphasis on targets and standards, alongside increasing expectations regarding involvement of service users, maintained the pressure towards greater accountability.

Section 3
What it's like to be accountable

When you know what your responsibilities are, and can carry them out, then being accountable can be a very satisfying state of affairs. Unfortunately, sometimes people don't know what they are responsible for, or, if they do, are not given the means to achieve it. Agencies often complain that they simply don't have enough resources to meet the performance targets set for them (e.g. Association of Metropolitan Authorities, 1993). This is investigated through the activities and case studies in this section.

3.1 Problems of accountability

The activities in this section involve using Offprint 32, *Problems of accountability: questionnaire.* The scope of questions is based on the items which appear in the box on 'structures of accountability' in Section 1.2 of this unit.

Activity 3

Allow about 15 minutes

Your problems of accountability

You will need Offprint 32 for this activity.

Retrieve your notes from Activity 1, where you considered some form of accountability you had experienced yourself. Then using this as an *aide-mémoire* tick whichever of the boxes in the first column of the questionnaire seem best to describe the situation you noted down previously. You can tick more than one box in each numbered block if that is appropriate. There won't be any comment on this activity, but the remainder of the section includes case study material which you can compare with your own response.

3.2 The case of Michael

Michael

Michael (not his real name) was employed as a care assistant in a private sector nursing home specialising in older clients with dementia. If these people were reluctant to go where the staff wanted them to, or if they wandered disruptively or were aggressive to other residents, it was common practice for staff to use physical means to restrain them or redirect them: for example by placing both hands on their shoulders and turning them around. Since the residents were frail relatively little force was required, but since they were frail even relatively little force might result in bruising or fracture. None of the care assistants appear to have had any training in this regard.

On one occasion a resident was poking another with a stick. Michael pulled her shoulder. Because of her osteoporosis this resulted in a fracture of the shoulder joint and the resident subsequently died of trauma. Michael reported what had happened to the proprietor, but the written report was made by the proprietor.

At the inquest Michael gave his account of the incident, but the care home proprietor read a written incident report which suggested that Michael had lost his temper with the resident. The coroner referred the case to the Crown Prosecution Service, but the CPS subsequently dropped it and the coroner returned a verdict of death by misadventure. The resident's relatives prepared a civil action against the nursing home. The civil action was dropped on legal advice when the nursing home proprietor showed he could demonstrate that the home had a written operational policy which forbade the use of physical restraint, claimed that Michael had been disobeying management guidance in this regard, and recited the incriminating incident report. Michael claimed that he had never seen the policy and that he had been misrepresented in the report. Michael was dismissed.

The local social services and health authority inspectors investigated the case, but did not withdraw registration. They were satisfied that the home had dismissed an unsuitable employee and in their report noted that the proprietor was putting an improved training scheme for care assistants into operation.

Activity 4   **Michael's accountability problem**

Allow about 5 minutes   Use the second column of boxes in the questionnaire to characterise Michael's accountability problem as shown in the case study box. You can believe his version of events for the purpose of this activity.

Comment   You probably ticked 1(a), insofar as Michael had not been given adequate instruction as to what the proprietor said was the home's policy on physical restraint, 2(a) insofar as it wasn't Michael who created the documentary evidence which counted, and especially 3(b), insofar as Michael was punished for doing something when he had not been given the instruction or the skill to do otherwise.

One of the interesting features of this case is the way it illustrates the allocation of blame between, on the one hand, an employee and, on the other, an organisation. Although in this case the organisation was actually the proprietor, in others it might be the management committee of a voluntary sector residential home, or the social services department in the case of a local authority home. In a broad sense, health and social care organisations are accountable for the safety and welfare of their clients (and their staff too): they have a legal *duty of care*. This duty extends to the actions of their staff if these were undertaken as part of their job. But how far this corporate responsibility extends depends on the interpretation of the legal concept of *vicarious liability*. Roughly speaking, organisations are not held responsible for damage done by their employees if this damage could not reasonably have been predicted or prevented by them. You will see that the term 'reasonable' appears in this formula, and terms like 'reasonable', 'appropriate' and 'suitable' appear throughout the Registered Homes Act 1984, and other health and care legislation too. What was *reasonable* under the circumstances (and what the circumstances really were) is difficult enough to decide, but to make matters more difficult, coroners, the criminal law, the civil law and inspection teams may well have different ideas about what would have been reasonable.

Activity 5   **Who cops the blame?**

Allow about 20 minutes   Some coloured pencils or highlighters will help with this activity since it asks you to trace routes through the maze of Figure 1 (overleaf). Use the case study of Michael to inspect the figure. The end point of the case was the sequence 12, 13, 16. Michael took all the blame for the incident. He was neither prosecuted nor sued for damages, but he was sacked and he will probably never work in care again.

(a)   Work your way back from point 12 to the beginning of the figure. Remember that it is not what really happened in the home which is important, but whose version gets believed. Through what route was point 12 reached in this case?

(b)   Now look at the figure from Michael's point of view. Suppose he was in a position to take his employer to an employment tribunal for unfair dismissal. How would he want the questions in the figure to be answered and where would he want the pathways to lead?

(c)   Now consider the resident's relatives. They decided not to sue Michael for damages, a very sensible decision given that Michael hadn't much money. But the care home proprietor was richer, was insured against such risks and had a legal duty of care, and there is a strong case for saying that he was negligent in this case. The relatives' case against the care home will be strengthened if they can demonstrate that the injury occurred because of organisational failings rather than because of individual malpractice. What route through the figure would their legal adviser try to achieve?

Comment   (a)   The actual route was 1, 3, 8, 12.

(b)   The route Michael might have preferred was 1, 3, 4, 6, 9, 13, 15 or 16. Ending at 15 might have strengthened his case since 16 leaves no one to blame in this case. But if he wanted reinstatement to his job, then 16 would have been preferable.

(c)   For the relatives 1, 2 and 14 would be the best route, but failing that 1, 3, 4, 6, 9, 13 and 15. The sequence 1, 3, 8, 12, 13 and 15 makes a less compelling case from the relatives' point of view since suggesting that Michael committed a criminal offence also implies he is the kind of person an employer could not reasonably be expected to control. Of course, if it could be proved that Michael already had a criminal record or history of violence, and the proprietor employed him knowing this, that would be a different matter.

There are three reasons why you were asked to do this activity. The first was to demonstrate what a tricky matter it can be to allocate blame between individuals and organisations. Both are accountable, but how each is brought to account and with what outcome depends very much on the actions of those who call them to account. In this case that means the actions of the doctor (who refused to sign the death certificate, thus provoking an inquest). Then there were the actions of the coroner, the police, the Crown Prosecution Service, the relatives and their legal advisers, the inspection team and, potentially, Michael bringing his employer to account for unfair dismissal and/or reporting him for perjury. This is highly characteristic of accountability in general. It is not something which is necessarily ever-present and which operates in a systematic way. Often whether people are brought to account, and for what and with what outcomes, is a very haphazard matter, as in this case.

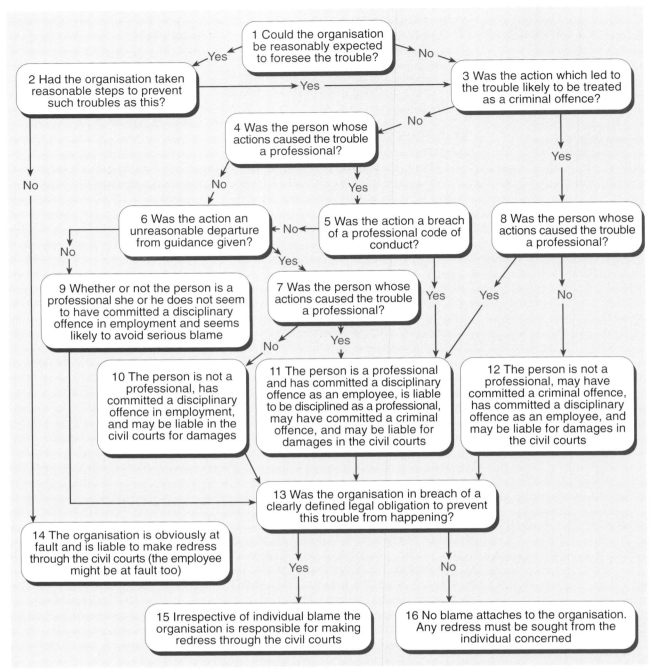

Figure 1 Considerations in deciding whether an employee or an employing organisation is at fault

Second, the case illustrates multiple systems of accountability characteristic of the health and care services. Workers are accountable:

- as individuals vulnerable to blame
- as members of organisations, making their agency blameworthy
- as employees and as employers in terms of employment law
- as citizens under criminal law
- to clients and their relatives in terms of contracts and/or the civil law
- to inspection units and regulatory bodies.

Although this didn't happen in the case study, the relatives might have held the inspection unit to account in various ways for its benign report on the home. If the resident's fees had been paid by social services they might have held the department accountable for placing their relative in an unsafe environment. Figure 1 also refers to professional accountability and that will be dealt with later.

Third, the case demonstrates the importance of documentary evidence in deciding such matters. There wasn't much, and what there was may have been falsified or misrepresented, but it still counted. The sources for this case study are Michael himself and a news cutting reporting the coroner's hearing. There can be no certainty as to whether Michael's account was accurate, but in reading the case your sympathies were probably with him rather than the proprietor, because it was his views which were put into a documentary form here. This links this unit with Unit 23, which discusses the connection between record making and accountability.

Key points

- Organisations are usually only legally responsible for problems which they could reasonably have been expected to predict and which they could have prevented by taking measures reasonable for them to take. But just what 'reasonable' means often has to be decided in court.

- People who work in health and social care contexts are usually involved in multiple structures of accountability. Which structure will come into play is often unpredictable.

- The investigation of records often determines who exactly was to blame, but that depends on what records there were to serve as evidence, and who made them.

3.3 Professional accountability

At the time that Michael was a care assistant, it was not one of the professional occupations for which practitioners' names are listed on a register licensing them to practise. Therefore, he could not call upon the network of support or the opportunity to develop professional skills as part of such an organisation. Equally, he could not be 'struck off' for failing to follow a professional code of practice or for having committed a criminal offence. However, this situation will change with the introduction of the General Social Care Council's register for social work and social care staff. Doctors, nurses, dentists and members of the professions allied to medicine (PAMs) such as occupational therapists, physiotherapists and chiropodists already have this additional type of accountability. Since doctors, nurses and dentists cannot pursue their occupation at all if they have been deregistered, and deregistered PAMs cannot be employed in the statutory services, this is a very serious kind of accountability. Had the proprietor of the home been a registered nurse, he might have found himself before the disciplinary committee of the Nursing and Midwifery Council. He might have been found guilty of a professional offence irrespective of what happened in the criminal or the civil courts, and struck off the register. Struck off, he could still have been a nursing home proprietor, but if he counted himself as part of the complement of registered nurses a nursing home has to have, he could not have acted in that capacity.

The next case study does feature professionals and professional accountability as well as accountability as employees of NHS trusts. It is about hospital nurses. Unlike Michael, those nurses seem to spend a great deal of time writing things down.

Activity 6   Accountability and risk

Allow about 20 minutes

For this activity turn to Chapter 31 in the Reader, by Ellen Annandale. It is an extract from a longer article of the same title (Annandale, 1996). Read the article, ticking the third column of the questionnaire (Offprint 32) appropriately as if you were answering for the nurses interviewed. In the course of your reading look out for what Annandale says about the discrepancy between these nurses' perceptions of risk and the reality of risk.

Comment   For the questionnaire you probably ticked 1(c), 2(c), 3(b), 3(c), 4(c) and 5(b). The overall impression is of a group of workers who feel oppressed and vulnerable to being the subject of complaints. These might be justifiable from the patients' point of view but from the nurses' view they would be more properly directed at the government, trust management, or sometimes at doctors rather than at nurses, because in the nurses' view they have been given responsibilities without being given adequate means to discharge them. You might have noted that one box which these nurses would certainly not tick would be 1(a). If anything, their responsibilities are all too clearly defined and the problem is that they feel they cannot do what they are regarded as being responsible for doing.

Annandale's comments on the reality and the perception of risk are interesting. Nurses make up the largest single category of employees in the NHS but they are only rarely the subject of formal complaints by patients and relatives. Data on complaints are not collated nationally, so it is difficult to be precise about figures. Moreover, whom a complaint is directed at and who it is decided is at fault are often different matters. It may be that fewer than 5 per cent of all formal complaints from patients and relatives are directed at nurses. Nurses are the subject of litigation in court only very rarely indeed (Annandale, 1996). The overwhelming majority of court cases involve doctors, directly or indirectly through a suit against a trust. But even a low rate of complaints against such a large group of workers generates enough news and gossip to worry the nurses. In fact, the most serious risk to nursing careers – although still a small one – comes from the disciplinary procedures of the nursing profession itself, and a very large proportion of these cases result from one nurse, as a manager, reporting another, as a subordinate, for professional misconduct. While the idea of professionalism suggests the autonomy for individual practitioners to exercise their discretion, in practice professionalism in nursing is often used as a means through which one group of nurses, as managers, regulates and restricts another group of nurses, as employees (Kellet, 1996).

3.4 Responsibilities without the means to discharge them

Feeling that you are accountable for doing what you don't think you can possibly do seems to be a rather common feature of accountability in some areas of health and social care. Authorities often claim that they cannot meet performance targets or their legal obligations because they don't have enough resources. Annandale's nurses don't feel that they are given the resources or support necessary to avoid the need for patients to complain. She refers to 'patients as a source of risk', meaning that nurses risk patients complaining. But sometimes practitioners are at risk from their clientele in a different sense – service users are likely to do what practitioners are supposed to prevent them from doing but don't have the powers or the resources for prevention. The next activity examines this issue.

Activity 7 **The case of Liam**

Allow about 10 minutes Liam (not his real name) is an approved social worker (he would be a mental health officer in Scotland, but Scottish mental health law is different). Under the terms of mental health legislation in England and Wales (Department of Health/Welsh Office, 1993) Liam has the power to recommend that someone should be compulsorily detained in hospital, if they are suffering from a mental disorder and if detention can be justified in the interests of:

- the person's health
- the person's safety
- the safety of other people.

The approved social worker's recommendation has to be supported by a doctor licensed to do so under the Mental Health Act 1983, usually a psychiatrist.

The social services department also has powers under Section 47 of the National Assistance Act 1948 to remove a person from insanitary living conditions and place them elsewhere against their will.

Now read the case study below and put yourself in Liam's position. What would you have done?

Liam

Mrs A was an older woman who caused considerable concern to her neighbours because she neglected herself and her property. Neighbours' concern resulted in one visit by the GP, two by the practice nurse and four by social workers over a period of three months. They were rarely admitted to the house and on each occasion Mrs A declined to accept any services offered. Liam was asked to visit. He gained entry to the house, which was sparsely furnished and cold, but relatively clean and with a proper water and electricity supply. Mrs A looked severely malnourished but was lucid and explained quite coherently that she didn't want other people interfering in her life.

Comment   Assuming you couldn't have been more persuasive than Liam, you might have considered the following.

1   It is doubtful whether conditions for using the provisions of the National Assistance Act obtained, since the house was not in an insanitary condition.

2   You might have considered initiating proceedings to have Mrs A committed to hospital under the terms of the Mental Health Act for assessment of her mental state, and to give her the benefits of hospital care. But Liam's powers depend on there being good evidence of mental illness and in his view she gave no indication of this.

3   You might have done nothing except to write a report indicating that the visit had been made, noting the circumstances found and your interpretation of these and, particularly, Mrs A's refusal of assistance.

What actually happened to Liam and Mrs A

In fact Liam took the last of the options described above. Some weeks later, following concern expressed by a neighbour, the police broke into Mrs A's house and found her dead. A coroner's inquiry found that she had died from self-neglect. The GP who gave evidence claimed 'it was obvious' that Mrs A was mentally ill and should have been committed to a psychiatric ward, and that she had originally referred the case to social services for this reason. The local newspapers ran headline stories about death by neglect on the part of social services, featuring interviews with the neighbours and the GP. Liam was suspended from duty on full pay, pending a confidential internal inquiry. He was completely exonerated since his actions were entirely consistent with mental health law, which is written precisely to make it difficult to undermine people's civil liberties by committing them to hospital against their will (Gomm, 1997). However, exoneration came after an agonising wait of three months and a loss of three months' service to the department.

So for Liam Mrs A constituted an accountability risk. You will have seen how in this case there was a conflict between, on the one hand, expectations for a social worker to prevent harm to a client and, on the other, the client's rights to privacy and self-determination. There are various areas of social care in which this kind of tension arises. For example, they arise with patients with dementia who 'wander' and thus endanger themselves and disturb other people's comfort and privacy, leading practitioners (and informal carers) to consider locked doors, electronic tags and worse. And they arise where social workers or health visitors are accused either of failing to detect and prevent child neglect or abuse, or alternatively of intruding unnecessarily into family life.

Key points

- Some agencies and workers in health and social care feel constrained in their practice because they believe that they are highly accountable but unable to fulfil their responsibilities because:
  - they don't have the necessary resources
    - working arrangements make it impossible
    - they don't have the legal powers
    - it would be an unethical infringement of civil liberties.

- Some workers in health and social care find themselves held accountable for actions of service users which they cannot practically or legally prevent.

Section 4
Responding to accountability

So far this unit has drawn attention to the difficulties some agencies and some workers in health and social care experience through being made accountable. So how do they respond to this? One kind of response is often called 'defensive practice'.

4.1 Defensive practice

The term 'defensive practice' is often used to refer to tactics employed by practitioners when at risk of being judged adversely. The best defensive practice is to do your job so well that no one has reason to complain about it, although the term 'defensive practice' is rarely used to mean that. One of the most prevalent responses in health and social care is 'to write everything down' in order to 'defend one's practice'. The news cutting opposite suggests that the increased tendency of people to complain about general practitioners has actually improved their practice in some respects.

Activity 8   Positive and negative features of defensive practice

Allow about 15 minutes   After reading the news cutting, which refers to research by Nicholas Summerton (1995), make two lists, one showing the benefits to patients of defensive practice, and the other the disadvantages to patients. This might not be as easy as it sounds.

Comment

Benefits to patients	Disadvantages to patients
More detailed note taking	More time on recording, less on treatment
More and better explanations to patients	Unnecessary prescriptions
More necessary diagnostic tests; risks justified by necessity for the tests	More unnecessary diagnostic tests with associated risks to patients
More necessary follow-ups	More unnecessary follow-ups
More necessary referrals	More unnecessary referrals
Less likely to do risky treatments in surgery	More likely to hospitalise patients who might safely have been treated in surgery
Practice audits	Striking off patients likely to complain or with difficult-to-treat conditions
	Much more costly practice

If your response is like the lists above, you will have realised that generalisations about whether these practices are beneficial or not won't necessarily apply to each and every patient. Thus, what might seem like an 'unnecessary' referral or an 'unnecessary' diagnostic test might in particular cases turn out to have been necessary, and what might seem like a procedure simple enough to carry out in the health centre might turn out to be very risky. This relates to another problem of accountability. Practitioners are accountable for assessing risks or assessing the benefits of treatment in advance, but only later know what the risks and benefits really were.

Defensive GPs 'help patients'

Chris Mihill Medical Correspondent

Doctors who carry out extra tests on patients in case they are sued may be giving the public a better service than those who do not, a researcher says today.

There has been concern about the alleged growth in Britain of 'defensive medicine' – whereby doctors carry out extensive and sometimes unnecessary tests to guard themselves against possible litigation – on the grounds that this wastes health service money and exposes patients to needless procedures.

But in a new survey, Nicholas Summerton, of Bradford Health Authority's department of public health medicine, says defensive medicine – particularly the more detailed explanation of what is to be done and more extensive note-taking of symptoms – can benefit patients.

Dr Summerton asked 300 general practitioners whether they had changed the way they worked for fear of complaints or legal action. Ninety-eight per cent said that they had made some practice changes in case a patient complained.

Around 60 per cent of the doctors said they were offering more diagnostic testing, more referrals to hospital, increased follow-ups and more detailed explanations. Some 40 per cent said they would avoid treating certain conditions in the surgery, and a similar proportion said they would consider extra diagnostic tests even where there was some risk to the patient.

Nearly 30 per cent said they would consider prescribing unnecessary drugs and 25 per cent said that they would remove patients from their list if they felt such patients were likely to complain.

Nine out of 10 of the doctors said they took more detailed notes and gave patients more detailed explanations, and a third said that they did more screening work or undertook practice audits to improve what they were doing.

Half the doctors said they were sometimes worried about being sued, and for 30 per cent this was a frequent worry. Just over 50 per cent said they were worried about a complaint being lodged with the family health services authority.

Dr Summerton, publishing the study in the British Medical Journal, says: 'Some defensive practices, such as more detailed note-taking, are clearly beneficial, but others will have adverse effects on both patient care and resource allocation.

'The existence of negative defensive medicine is perhaps best viewed as a symptom of the fundamental problems inherent within the present regulatory systems.'

Dr Summerton says that proposed changes to the complaints system will lead to an increase in complaints, and a corresponding rise in defensive practices which will not benefit patients.

(*Guardian*, 7 January 1995)

"It's not the risk to you I'm worried about. It's the risk to my career that bothers me."

Not all practitioners are in a position to respond to increased accountability by doing their job better, or by doing it in a way which is more pleasing to those to whom they are accountable. Then defensive practice can become a serious problem.

The range of tactics includes the following.

- Practitioners give as few undertakings as possible, make few promises, do not give service users predictions of what might happen, withhold from service users information about what they have a right to expect – on the grounds that the less they promise, the less people will complain about.

- They do not inform service users of their rights to complain, or they make complaining difficult. In the case of some GPs featured in the news cutting, they get rid of patients most likely to complain (Patients Association, 1996).

- They make records in such a way as to show that correct procedures were followed, even if they were not. Falsified records are quite common in negligence claims, compounding the offence if this is discovered.

- They make very extensive records just in case they are needed to rebut some accusation which is unpredictable at the time. Annandale's nurses employed this tactic.

- They practise out of sight of colleagues, superiors, or others who might give testimony to poor practice. The care assistants in the Reader chapter by Lee-Treweek, 'Bedroom abuse', are an example (Units 4 and 8).

- They practise in a way that limits the opportunities for service users to do anything a practitioner might get blamed for; in effect, they practise more coercively. After swinging in favour of more autonomy for mental health service users, the pendulum may now be swinging back the other way (Gomm, 1997).

As suggested in this unit, the first two of these tactics were more characteristic of health and social care up to the 1990s. They became rather more difficult to follow in the 1990s, so practitioners may be thrown back on the following tactics.

- They do things which are unnecessary but which, if not done, might lead to a complaint. This is often used as an explanation for why so many operations are performed in the USA, where patients are very ready to sue (Berliner, 1997). There were indications of this in the news cutting.

- They avoid doing something which might be beneficial but may be misunderstood or misrepresented. For example, many male primary school teachers or childcare workers avoid physical contact with the children they care for in the wake of public scandals about child abuse. Many first-aiders are now reluctant to assist at accidents given a spate of court cases against St John Ambulance and Red Cross volunteers.

- They never make a risky decision all by themselves. They always involve service users, colleagues and superiors in decision making. Then, if things go wrong, there will be a large number of people forced to support them (Tilley, 1996).

Conclusion

There were three core questions for this unit. The first of these was:

- **What does it mean to be accountable?**

In Section 1 you saw what accountability means. You also looked at the various directions in which people could be accountable and the various mechanisms used to bring them to account. Then in Section 3 you saw how being accountable can put you in a very uncomfortable position. You may find yourself held accountable for not having done things which you could not, under the circumstances, do; or you may be vulnerable to blame for things you could not have avoided.

The second question was:

- **Why has there been pressure to increase the level of accountability in health and social care?**

In Section 2 you read about the development of assertive consumerism among those who use health and care services (e.g. the self-advocacy group you met in Unit 22). You also read about the increase in central government control over local health and social services, leading to increased control by managers over health and social care workers. The broader background in which demands for more accountability have developed is discussed in Block 7.

The third core question was:

- **What problems arise for people and agencies who are made accountable and how do they respond to these?**

In Sections 3 and 4 you saw that problems of accountability arise when it is unclear what people's responsibilities are, when they have responsibilities they are not able to fulfil, and when they are accountable in one direction for doing one thing, and in another direction for doing the opposite. Reducing accountability was probably not an option in the late 1990s given the groundswell of support for increasing it at that time, nor probably would it be desirable. Of course, many practitioners could be relied upon if they were treated as trustworthy and allowed more autonomy. But without some system of accountability it is not easy to distinguish those who can be trusted from those who cannot.

In Section 4 you read about 'defensive practice': the responses made by people in the face of difficult situations of accountability. As you saw, some defensive practice is good practice insofar as it avoids complaint by giving people nothing to complain about. But the right balance has to be found. Occasionally taking accountability too far into the direction of service users may mean doing what they want even if it does them harm. This would not be 'accountability' in the end. There is an ethical issue here about whose opinion should prevail in such circumstances: the service user's or the practitioner's. And sometimes defensive practice means wheeling and dealing, ducking and diving, to make sure that wherever the blame falls, it doesn't fall on you. When people are accountable for achieving what it is impossible for them to achieve, the latter is often their only defence.

References

Althuser (1971) *Lenin and Philosophy and Other Essays*, New Left Books, London.

Annandale, E. (1996) 'Working on the front-line: risk culture and nursing in the new NHS', *Sociological Review*, Vol. 44, No. 3, pp. 416–51.

Association of Metropolitan Authorities (1993) *Mental Health Services: Issues for Local Government*, AMA, London.

Audit Commission (1995) *Local Authority Performance Indicators*, Vol. 1, Vol. 2 and Appendix to Volumes 1 and 2, Audit Commission, London.

Berliner, D. (1997) 'Law of averages', *Health Service Journal*, 20 March, pp. 30–31.

Brindle, D. (1997) 'Key court victory for child carers', *Guardian*, 1 February, p. 7.

Brochie, J. and Wann, M. (1993) *Training for Lay Participation in Health*, Patients Association, London.

Combes, R. (1995) 'Caring league prompts point scoring fears', *Care Weekly*, 30 March, p. 1.

Cooper, L., Coote, A., Davies, A. and Jackson, C. (1995) *Voices Off: Tackling the Democratic Deficit in Health*, Institute for Public Policy Research, London.

Department of Health (1996) *Coordinating Community Mental Health Care*, Department of Health/The Open University, Milton Keynes.

Department of Health Social Services Inspectorate (1994) *Complaints Procedures in Local Authority Social Services Departments: Second Overview Report*, Chief Inspector's letter (94) 28, Department of Health, London.

Department of Health/Welsh Office (1993) *Mental Health Act 1983: Code of Practice*, HMSO, London/Cardiff.

Gomm, R. (1997) 'Supervision Registers' and 'Community Supervision' in The Open University, K257 *Mental Health and Distress: Perspectives and Practice, Offprints Book*, pp. 68–72.

Gordon, R. (1993) *Community Care Assessments: A Practical Legal Framework*, Longman, Harlow.

Harris, J. (1996) 'Peace deals', *Health Service Journal*, 16 May, Special Law Report, pp. 1–5.

Hogg, C. (1996) *How Do I Make a Complaint?*, Patients Association, London.

www.doh.gov.uk

Jones, A., Jeyasingham, D. and Rajasooriya, S. Invisible families: The strengths and needs of Black families in which young people have caring responsibilities, The Policy Press, www.jrf.org.uk/ [accessed: 24.7.02]

www.jrf.org.uk/knowledge/findings/socialcare/412.asp [accessed: 24.7.02]

Kellet, J. (1996) 'A nurse suspended', *British Medical Journal*, Vol. 313, pp. 1249–50.

Kumar, S. (1997) *Accountability: Relationships Between the Voluntary Sector 'Providers', Local Government 'Purchasers' and Service Users in the Contract State*, Joseph Rowntree Foundation/York Publishing Services, York.

McKechnie, S. (1996b) 'Consumer groups', in Merry (1996) pp. 252–56.

Mihill, C. (1995) 'Defensive GPs "help patients"', *Guardian*, 7 January.

National Association of Health Authorities and Trusts (1997) *A Measure of Effectiveness? A Critical Review of the NHS Efficiency Index*, NAHAT, Birmingham.

O'Neill, O. (2002) *A Question of Trust – Called to Account*, Reith Lectures 2002, BBC Radio 4.

Ogden, J. (1996) 'Open court', *Health Service Journal*, 9 May, pp. 12–13.

Patients Association (1996) 'Are you an expensive patient? Are you a 'nuisance'? Are you struck off? Can we help?', *Patients' Voice*, Autumn, p. 2.

Public Law Project (1994) *Is It Lawful? A Guide to Judicial Reviews*, Public Law Project/Unison, London.

Reith Lectures (2002) BBC.

RNIB, Priorities in health and social care for blind and partially sighted people, www.rnib.org.uk/campaign/welcome.htm [accessed: 24.6.02] www.rnib.org.uk/campaign/improvelives/report.htm [accessed: 24.6.02]

Scottish Consumer Council/Scottish Association of Health Councils (1992) *Patients' Rights: GP and Hospital Services*, Scottish Consumer Council, Glasgow.

Summerton, N. (1995) 'Positive and negative features in defensive medicine: a questionnaire study of general practitioners', *British Medical Journal*, Vol. 310, pp. 27–9.

The Open University (1992) B789 *Managing Voluntary and Non-profit Enterprises*, The Open University, Milton Keynes.

Tilley, J. (1996) 'Accounts, accounting and accountability in psychiatric nursing' in Watson, R. (ed.) *Accountability in Nursing Practice*, Chapman and Hall, London.

Wallcraft, J. (1993) 'Empowering empowerment: professionals and self-advocacy projects', *Journal of Mental Health Nursing*, Vol. 14, No. 2, pp. 7–9.

Acknowledgements

Grateful acknowledgement is made to the following sources for permission to reproduce material in this unit:

Text

Ogden, J. (1996) 'Open court', *Health Service Journal*, 9 May, © Joy Ogden 1996; Spiers, J. and Howland, G. (1996) 'Your patients association – We are here to listen, call us with your stories', *Patients' Voices*, No. 1, The Patients Association; Mihill, C. (1995) 'Defensive GPs "help patients"' *The Guardian*, 7 January, © Guardian Newspapers Ltd.

Illustrations/Photographs

p.100 (right): NHS Citizens' Charter: Complaints: Listening ... Acting ... Improving (1996), NHS Executive, Department of Health; *p.100 (left and middle)* Courtesy of Hertfordshire County Council.

Unit 25
Letting the Right People Know

Originally prepared for the course team by Roger Gomm
Revised by Danielle Turney and Marion Reichart

While you are working on Unit 25, you will need:

- Course Reader
- *The Good Study Guide*
- Wallchart
- *Getting a Vocational Qualification: A Student's Guide*

Contents

Introduction

Unit 25 focuses on:

- making confidentiality policy accessible to clients

- putting confidentiality policy into practice

- developing your writing skills – in particular report writing

- working with numbers – scatter diagrams

- preparing for the examination.

This is the sixth of the K100 skills units. The first (Unit 5) outlined five principles which should underpin good practice in social and health care. These were:

1   enable people to develop their own potential

2   enable people to have a voice and be heard

3   respect people's beliefs and preferences

4   promote and support people's rights to appropriate services

5   respect people's privacy and rights to confidentiality.

As you know, each of the skills units has focused on one of these value statements. This unit focuses on the last by dealing with the duty of confidentiality and how to put it into practice. It continues work you began in Unit 23 using the NIAS confidentiality policy. This makes Unit 25 less self-contained than the other skills units. It is also relatively brief. This is because you have already done some important skills work through the activities in Unit 23 (particularly Activities 8, 9, 10 and 11). Unit 25 recognises that you already have some familiarity with applying a confidentiality policy and builds on that. It also continues work with your study skills. In Section 3 you will find activities on managing your K100 filing system; numerical and graphical skills centred on reading scatter diagrams; report writing skills; and preparing for the end of year exam.

Central themes of the unit

A key theme of this block has been the importance of information and the way it is gathered, recorded and shared. Much of the information involved in health and social care refers to matters which service users would prefer not to broadcast widely. Unit 23 included a great deal of material on privacy and confidentiality, and Section 1 of this unit keeps to the same themes. The K100 skills units deal with topics in a practical way, to help you recognise and develop the skills which are needed for competent work in health and social care. In this unit you will build on the skills you started using in Unit 23, and think further about the kinds of decisions which people in health and social care really do make when they apply a confidentiality policy to the situations which arise in the course of their work.

Section 1
Putting a confidentiality policy into practice

In Unit 23 you looked at how confidentiality policies work by exploring the implications of the policy of a fictional drugs agency NIAS. We now return to NIAS to look at the more practical implications of putting a confidentiality policy into practice.

1.1 Making a confidentiality policy accessible to service users

The NIAS confidentiality policy (Offprint 30) was written for people who work in the agency, whether as paid workers or volunteers. Although there is no reason why service users should not read it, it is not the kind of document most service users would feel inclined to read. Yet the policy itself requires service users to be told what the policy is (clause 12), which implies being told in a straightforward and understandable way. The principles of accessibility are the same as those discussed in Unit 22 about communicating with service users in ways they can easily understand.

Activity 1 **Presenting the NIAS policy to service users**

Allow about 30 minutes

For this activity write a simple 'service user-friendly' statement of the NIAS confidentiality policy which could be stuck on the wall of the waiting room, the notice board etc. Make sure it:

- is brief, but contains the main information that service users need to know
- is suitable for display as a poster (i.e. in large lettering) on the wall of the agency
- is written in everyday language, without distorting the content of the policy
- addresses what you think will be service users' major concerns (of course, if you were doing this 'for real' you would be able to ask them what their main concerns were)
- tells them that they can ask a member of staff to explain the policy more fully
- informs them of their right to complain if they think their confidentiality has been breached.

You will need to look at the NIAS confidentiality policy again in Offprint 30 and pick out the essential points. You might want to go through highlighting them first before trying to summarise them.

You could also check back to pages 23-27 of Unit 22 to remind yourself about designing user friendly communications.

Comment There are lots of ways you could select and organise key points from the policy. If you were doing it for real, you could try out different versions with a group of clients to get their views on how to get the main messages across. On the next page you can see my effort at this task.

Can you trust us with your secrets?

NIAS has a strict confidentiality policy. You have a right to expect members of NIAS staff to treat all information about you as CONFIDENTIAL. This means that:

* members of NIAS staff will ONLY pass on information about you to OTHER members of NIAS staff if they definitely NEED to know in order to carry out their work

* members of NIAS staff will NOT pass information about you to ANYONE outside NIAS, without your permission.

This applies to:

* anything you say to any member of NIAS staff

* anything you say in a NIAS workshop, or other group meeting

* anything said about you by your friends or others

* any information about you that might come to a member of NIAS staff from any other source.

Very occasionally we have to make an exception to this rule because:

* a COURT orders us to disclose information about you

* there is SERIOUS RISK to a child's welfare, or to someone's safety

* you are not in a position to give your permission.

But even in these cases:

* permission to pass on the information has to be given by the Director of NIAS after consultation with staff and

* we would, if at all possible, talk to you first about passing on the information.

If at any time you suspect that confidential information about you has been wrongly passed on by NIAS staff, you can make a complaint, which will be fully investigated. To make a complaint ask to see...

If you want to find out more about this confidentiality policy, ask the member of NIAS staff you are in contact with.

1.2   Acting on a breach of confidentiality

With your user-friendly version of the policy pinned up on the agency walls, you hope that your clients will now be clear about their rights to confidentiality. But what if a breach of confidentiality occurs? How should you respond? And how should you make a record of the breach, so that it could be followed up and appropriate action taken?

A breach of Wayne's confidentiality

Pat Walsh is a regular volunteer at NIAS. One of her jobs is to co-lead a weekly group meeting, the Wednesday Group, for some of the service users. One afternoon, she walks into the kitchen and overhears a conversation between Jonti and Michelle. They are discussing a group session that both Jonti and Wayne had attended. Pat realises that they are discussing something that Wayne had disclosed in the group, which she knows he wanted to keep confidential. When Michelle leaves, a few moments later, Pat speaks to Jonti. He asks her something further about Wayne, but she makes it clear that she cannot talk about Wayne to him. Jonti acknowledges his breach of confidentiality but says that he only told Michelle — and anyway she and Wayne are friends and he thought that Wayne would be OK about her knowing. Pat reminds him that he has no permission to pass on information in this way and refers him to the agency's confidentiality policy.

Activity 2   **Reporting a breach of confidentiality**

Allow about 45 minutes

A couple of days later, Marion (the Director of NIAS) asks Pat whether she knows anything about a breach of confidentiality as Wayne has made a complaint to her, claiming that one of the service users has passed on information about him.

Imagine that you are Pat and that Marion has asked you to prepare a brief report on the situation, outlining what happened and any action you have taken.

Before writing the report, look again at clauses 1,12 and 18 of the confidentiality policy in the Offprint Book. You will also need to look ahead to Section 3.3 and read quickly through the second part which outlines what you should try to achieve in a report. A report should be brief, focused, written to serve a purpose and written for the right audience. Try to give a clear account of the incident, say how you responded, and why you did what you did. Refer to the clauses of the report that are relevant to the case. Although the report should be concise, remember that Marion was not there, so will only know what you tell her about your involvement in the incident.

Comment   There is no single correct way of writing this report, but certain points will need to be included. You should also have made sure you referred to the clauses of the policy that are relevant to this case.

You can see my version of the report on the next page.

> **REPORT**
>
> To: Marion Smith, Director
>
> From: Pat Walsh, volunteer and co-leader of Wednesday Group
>
> Re: Breach of confidentiality

Background

I was working at NIAS on Wednesday 12 June and had spent the morning in the 'Wednesday Group'; both Jonti and Wayne attend regularly and both were there that morning. After the group finished, everyone went off for lunch.

The incident

After lunch, at about 2.30, I went into the kitchen to make a drink. When I went in, I noticed that Jonti and Michelle were over by the sink. They were talking together; no-one else was in the room. Jonti glanced over and said 'hi' to me and continued with his conversation. I was not trying to listen, but Jonti did not lower his voice much and I could hear what he was saying. He seemed to be in the middle of a discussion with Michelle, telling her about something he had heard. I realised that he was talking about Wayne and repeating something that Wayne had discussed in the Group earlier that day. I was quite taken aback, because Wayne had found it difficult to talk about this issue and had only done so when he had been reassured that it would be confidential to the group.

Action taken

In clause 18 in the Confidentiality Policy, it says that if members of the agency are aware of staff or service users disclosing confidential information about others then they should draw attention to what is happening. So I went over to Jonti and asked him if I could have a word. I did not want to talk to Jonti in front of Michelle.

Michelle then left the kitchen and I spoke to Jonti. I told him that I could not help overhearing some of his conversation, and said that it sounded like he had been talking about Wayne. He agreed that he had, and said that he had been concerned about Wayne, following the Group discussion. He asked me about one of the things Wayne said, but I told him that I could not discuss information about Wayne with him (clause 1). I reminded him that we had all agreed that anything said in the Group was Confidential – and that this was also what the Confidentiality Policy said. I confirmed that he had been given a copy of the Confidentiality Policy when he started to come to NIAS (clause 12), and that he had agreed to keep to it. I told him that Wayne would be entitled to complain if he believed that his confidentiality had been breached (clause 12). Jonti did not seem too bothered, and said that he had only told Michelle, and he was sure that Wayne would not mind as they were friends. He did say that he had not checked with Wayne first, though. I reminded him again that he had no right to pass on information about Wayne and that he needed to make sure that he kept to the policy in future.

Signed: Pat Walsh

14 June 2002

1.3 To disclose or not to disclose? A tricky question

To bring your work on confidentiality to a close, we will return to a question that was first raised in Unit 23: under what circumstances is it right to disclose confidential information? Policies do not always tell you clearly what to do, as we saw in the case of Michelle. And sometimes they may even appear to indicate actions which seem unwise under the particular circumstances. In such situations the question to ask is: 'Would more harm come from keeping matters confidential than from disclosing them?' Activity 3 invites you to ask this question about the scenario below.

A stabbing on Christmas Eve

On Christmas Eve Marion, the director of NIAS, was talking to a client in the agency. Another client came in and an argument started between the two. The first client stabbed the newcomer and then ran away. Marion administered first aid to a flesh wound in the upper arm and then took the injured client to A&E. The client who carried out the stabbing was on parole and, if his probation officer were told of the event, this would probably result in his being returned to prison and being charged with an additional offence. The dispute was about some illegal business and the client who was stabbed was insistent that the matter should not be reported to the police.

NIAS has no contractual obligation to the probation service to report to them on the behaviour of its clients.

Activity 3

Allow about 30 minutes

Trouble on Christmas Eve

(a)   Look at the NIAS confidentiality policy (clause 5b in particular), and list the options it allows Marion to take.

(b)   Fill in the grid below.

	Harm which might be done by keeping the information confidential	**Harm which might be done by disclosing the information**
To the agency		
To the worker		
To the client who did the stabbing		
To the client who was stabbed		
To the probation service		
To the public		

(c)   Decide what Marion should have done. The policy itself does not provide a right answer.

(d)   Marion will have to record this incident in an incident book, and report on it to the management committee of NIAS. Imagine that you are Marion and write a brief report to the management committee describing what happened, indicating your decision, and justifying it. In order to justify the decision you will need to show the options available (question (a) above) and say why you chose the option(s) you did and rejected the others. Before you write your report have a look at clause 17 of the confidentiality policy in the Offprint Book.

Comment   I am not going to give you my own answer to this activity. In some years you will find that it is an option you can take up for TMA 06. If not it is up to you decide whether you will find it useful to practise this skill and keep your report in your K100 portfolio.

Section 2
Consolidating your practice learning

The activities in Unit 23 Section 3 and in the section you have just finished, have given you opportunities to work with a particular confidentiality policy. However, they also involved you in other types of task which are common in health and social care: see Table 1.

Table 1 Common tasks for care workers

What you did	Unit 23 Activity No.				Unit 25 Activity No.		
	8	9	10	11	1	2	3
Read and interpreted a policy or code of practice	√	√	√	√	√	√	√
Explained a policy or code of practice to others					√		
Made a considered and justifiable judgement where a policy or code of practice gave no definitive guidance			√				√
Wrote a report for a particular readership						√	√
Wrote some information materials for service users					√		

2.1 Reviewing your learning

The knowledge and skills you have gained in relation to managing confidentiality have wider application and can be transferred to different areas of practice. Indeed, the ability to transfer learning from one context to another is a skill in itself, and one worth developing. Within some areas of health and social care (social work, for example) the ability to transfer learning appropriately is a key element of professional competence. The activity below asks you to review what you have learnt and to consider how it might be transferred to other health or social care practices.

Activity 4   **Reviewing transferable learning**

Allow about 15 minutes   For this activity fill in the grid overleaf or draw your own, bigger, version if necessary. In the first column write down what you think you learnt about confidentiality practice from this unit. In the second column write down how you think the learning could be transferred. For example, interpreting confidentiality policies is very similar to interpreting other policies or codes of practice. In the last column try to identify any further knowledge or any further opportunities for practice you need to gain. If you are aiming for a

VQ then you should do this last part of the activity with the advice of your mentor and with the standards for your VQ scheme beside you.

What you did	What did you learn about confidentiality practice in particular?	To what other practices could the learning be transferred?	What more do you need to know/practise?
Interpreted a policy document			
Explained a policy to others			
Made a justifiable judgement where the policy gave no definitive guidance			
Wrote a report			
Wrote information for service users			

2.2 Adding to your K100 portfolio

The activities shown in Table 2 are probably suitable for a VQ portfolio, but to establish this you will need to read the VQ assessment scheme relevant to you, as advised in *Getting a vocational qualification*.

Table 2 Portfolio activities

Unit 25 Activity number	End Product	Demonstrates competence in:
1	Text suitable for display as a poster	• Interpreting written policy • Explaining a written policy to others • Writing materials suitable for service users
2	Report to agency director or line manager	• Interpreting written policy • Writing a report for a particular readership
3	Report to management committee	• Interpreting written policy • Making a judgement where policy provides no definitive guidance • Writing a report for a particular readership

Anyone reading your portfolio will need to know what the items in it represent. None of these items makes much sense without the NIAS confidentiality policy, so you will need to photocopy that to include in your portfolio. You will also need to provide an explanation of the tasks that generated the different items. For this you could simply make copies of the activity instructions, or you could find another way of explaining what these items resulted from. And none of them makes much sense in *portfolio terms* unless you say what skills or competences each item is evidence of. One way of expressing this is in the last column of Table 2. But be careful if you are designing a portfolio for a particular assessment scheme. Each scheme will have its own vocabulary for describing skills or competences, and you will need to use the terms current in that scheme.

Section 3
Study skills

3.1 Keeping your K100 filing system in shape

With all this talk about records and their uses, what do *you* actually do with your own written records of your studies (your notes and TMAs)? Can you find your way to what you need – or has your course work become just a big pile? Every student needs an effective filing system. In many ways your filing system is more important than your memory. Nobody remembers everything, but clever students can find their way to *what* they need to know *when* they need to know it. However, filing isn't easy. A complicated system can be self-defeating, too time-consuming and too hard to remember. You need something fairly simple and also flexible (so that you aren't left with lots of pieces of paper which don't fit anywhere). But when you start working in a new area, you can't easily tell what shape of filing system is going to work well. Generally it's best to start with a very obvious and simple system and then modify it as you go along.

Have you modified any of your K100 files? What labels do you currently have on your folders? When did you last bring your files up to date? Is it time to do some reorganising and relabelling? (A supply of sticky labels can be very useful. If your files are easy to relabel, you are more likely to get round to doing it.)

It isn't *just* a matter of ensuring quick access to information. Organising your files is a way of making yourself think about how the course is organised. By the time you have worked out an effective filing system for your course notes, you have learned something pretty fundamental about the nature and content of the course.

3.2 Reading scatter diagrams

In K100 you have mainly looked at numbers presented in the form of tables, bar charts and pie charts. Now you will see another way of presenting them – as a scatter diagram (sometimes scattergram for short). You can see an example in Figure 1 overleaf. The particular numbers you will focus on are to do with the allocation of resources for mental health care to different districts of London. As you might expect, districts vary in the need for mental health care.

> *The need for mental health care varies widely with local characteristics, particularly with social deprivation, leading to a four or fivefold difference in the need for resources in different areas ... Hospital admission rates for different populations – a good 'proxy' for need – vary by a factor of five and are associated with social factors such as the number of people living alone and in poverty. A reasonably accurate way of predicting admission rates is based on Brian Jarman's underprivileged area scores – the so-called Jarman 8, which combines eight of these social factors.*
>
> *(Audit Commission, 1994, p. 10)*

Activity 5   Hospital admission rates and the Jarman 8 index

Allow about 10 minutes   (a)   What do you think is meant by hospital admission rates being a "good 'proxy' for need"? Why would you want a proxy?

(b)   What does the Jarman 8 index measure?

Comment   (a)   The need for health care in different localities is a complicated (and therefore expensive) thing to measure, whereas when people are admitted to hospital their home address and the nature of their need are routinely recorded. So hospital admissions records offer data which can be analysed to see, for each local district, how many people are admitted for mental health care. These admission rates can then be used as a 'proxy' for fully researched estimates of local need. (This is similar to a proxy vote, where someone votes on behalf of someone else.) But admission rates certainly are not a perfect measure of local need. For example, some people who need mental health care do not seek it, possibly because they are not aware of their need; others pay for private treatment. However, the authors of the Audit Commission report tell us that hospital admission rates are a 'good' proxy for need (on the basis of previous research comparing admission rates with other measures of need for treatment).

(b)   The Jarman index is a measure of how socially deprived an area is. It is obtained by combining figures for eight social factors (such as numbers of people living alone and in poverty). According to the Audit Commission report, the Jarman score for an area is a good predictor of admission rates to hospitals: if you know the Jarman score for an area, you can make a good guess at how many people will be admitted to hospital for mental health problems. So the Jarman score is also a good indicator of the level of need for mental health care.

The Audit Commission was interested in whether the level of *need* for mental health care in different London districts bears any relationship to how much is *spent* on mental health care in those districts. They took as their measure of need the Jarman score for each district.

Study skills: Figures that stand for figures

So the Jarman score is used because it is a good predictor of hospital admissions rates, which are a good proxy for mental health care needs. It is a figure standing for a figure which stands for another figure. Social scientists have to be flexible and cunning in making use of the data available. Time and cost impose severe constraints. You are seldom in a position to get exactly the figures you want, but you may be able to get a pretty good estimate by working from other figures.

Look now at Figure 1. You can see why diagrams like this are called scatter diagrams. It is because they show how some things are scattered or distributed. The dots which are scattered on the diagram are health districts. If this were a map, you would read it to see how health districts were scattered in space: north, south, east and west of each other. But in this case the diagram shows how the districts are distributed, on the one hand in terms of how much they spend on mental health services, and on the other in terms of the local need for mental health services. This is still a kind of mapping, but not in terms of spatial positions.

- First look at the horizontal line (called the 'horizontal axis'). It shows Jarman scores ranging from –40 (low need) at the left to 80 (high need) at the right.

- Then look at the vertical line (or vertical axis). It shows expenditure on mental health, ranging from £180 per head (per annum) to £0.

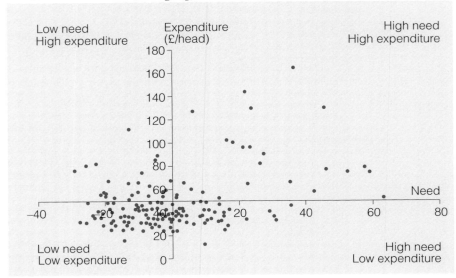

Figure 1 The relationship between need for mental health care and expenditure in London districts (Audit Commission, 1994, p. 12, 'Exhibit 6')

Activity 6

Allow about 5 minutes

Interpreting a scatter diagram 1

(a) How high, roughly, is the highest expenditure per head on mental health care?

(b) How low, roughly, is the lowest expenditure?

(c) What, roughly, is the highest Jarman score of any district?

(d) What, roughly, is the lowest Jarman score of any district?

(e) Can you see what the average expenditure per head is?

Comment

(a) About £165 per head per annum. You need to find the highest dot on the diagram (up and towards the right). This dot stands for the district with the highest expenditure. If you look left from the dot to the vertical axis you will see it is just slightly above 160 but not as far as half-way to 180. You can't do better than a rough guess of about 165.

(b) About £10–15 per head. The lowest dot is just to the right of the vertical axis. You can see that the dot is below 20, but not as far as half-way down to 0.

(c) About 63–64 is my estimate. You are looking for the dot furthest over to the right. It is just above the horizontal axis. Remember this high score means the district is very needy.

(d) Getting towards –30. That is the dot furthest over to the left – standing for the district with the least need.

(e) Nearly £50 per head. The horizontal axis cuts across the vertical axis between 40 and 60 – say 48. (The average Jarman score is 0.) Not all scatter diagrams allow you to read off an average in this way – it depends how the axes are drawn.

Don't worry if you found question (e) difficult to answer.

You now have the general gist of what this diagram is about. It shows districts of London, represented as dots, and the position of each dot shows how much was spent per head in that district and how needy it is.

Activity 7   **Interpreting a scatter diagram 2**

Allow about 5 minutes   (a)   Are there districts which have high need and which also spend a lot on mental health care?

(b)   Are there districts which have high need but don't spend much on mental health care?

(c)   Do the districts with the lowest need spend least on mental health care?

(d)   Is there a relationship between the level of need in districts and the amount they spend on mental health care?

Comment   (a)   The seven dots which are furthest over to the right (highest need) are all above the horizontal line (above average expenditure). Also the five highest dots (highest spending) are to the right of the vertical line (above average need). In fact all the districts which fall in the top-right part of the diagram are above average for both need and spending. So the answer is – yes, there are a lot of districts with high need which spend a lot.

(b)   There are many dots which fall to the right of the vertical line (some with need scores nearly as high as 40) and also below the horizontal line (below average expenditure). So the answer is – yes, there are districts with high need which don't spend much.

(c)   There are some dots well to the left (low need) which are also well above the horizontal line (above average expenditure). In fact, although there are plenty of low-need districts which are below average spenders (bottom left), there are also plenty which are above average (top left). So – no, you can't say that the districts with the lowest need spend least.

(d)   If there were a very clear relationship between need and spending, the dots would tend to fall in a straight line running from bottom left to top right. In other words, the higher the need score, the higher the spending score; and the lower the need score, the lower the spending score. But these dots are scattered all over the place. They don't look at all like a straight line. So there is certainly not a strong relationship between the two. However, the fact that there are no dots in the far top left, or the far bottom right, indicates a slight relationship.

When a scatter diagram like this shows the dots all tending to fall close to a line from bottom left to top right, then it shows a strong *correlation*.

Study skills: Scatter diagrams and correlations

You came across correlations near the end of Section 3.1 of Unit 19. A correlation means that two things vary together. For example, taller people tend to be heavier. So height and weight are correlated; but not perfectly, because some short people are heavy and some tall people are light. Correlations are often expressed as a number – a correlation coefficient. A perfect positive correlation is expressed as 1.0. It hardly ever happens in reality. Negative correlations are also possible. For example, the vertical position of the two ends of a see-saw shows a perfect negative correlation (-1.0) because however high up one end is, the other end must be a corresponding distance down. Perfect negative correlations hardly ever happen either. Coefficients greater than 0.8 or less than -0.8 are taken to indicate very strong correlations; 0.5 and -0.5 are fairly strong correlations. Zero indicates no correlation at all. On the diagram you have been looking at there is a very weak positive correlation between expenditure and need, probably around 0.1.

You will not need to go any further with scatter diagrams and correlations in K100. You don't need to know how to create a scatter diagram, or how to do the statistics necessary to calculate a correlation. But it is useful to know what to look for in scatter diagrams, because they crop up in books and articles about health and social care.

Up to a point you can see whether there is a correlation shown on a scatter diagram. If there is a strong one, most of the dots will fall close to a diagonal line, running bottom left to top right for a positive correlation, or top left to bottom right for a negative one. If the dots are more scattered around, but you can see that they fall roughly in an oval shape which tilts from bottom left to top right of the diagram, then there is a correlation – but a weaker one.

So what have you found out by working on this diagram? Basically, it shows that although the need for mental health care is a great deal higher in some districts of London than others, and although spending per head is 10 times as high in some districts as in others, there is very little relationship between level of need and spending. Some districts (top left) with relatively low need are spending quite a lot, and, more worryingly, some (bottom right) with high need are spending relatively little.

3.3 Developing your writing

As you approach your last TMA, it is time to review your writing skills. Do you feel you have made significant progress since February? And how do you feel in general now about the writing aspect of study?

Feelings about writing

Study skills: The intensity of writing

Do you look forward to writing, dread it, or simply resign yourself to it? Or is it a love/hate relationship – tremendously demanding, but also very rewarding to look back on? It would be quite surprising if it were something you treated lightly. Most people feel as if writing puts them through an emotional wringer. Why is this? And, as a student with perhaps several more years of writing ahead of you, can you cope with such intensity?

Activity 8

Allow about 30 minutes

Read Section 6, 'The experience of writing', in Chapter 6 of *The Good Study Guide*.

Then answer these questions. They correspond to the sub-sections of Section 6, so you may want to check back to the text as you think about them:

(a) Do you sometimes feel that your writing makes you appear a bit stupid and inarticulate?

(b) When you weigh up the quality of your writing, whose writing do you think you are comparing yourself against?

(c) Do you feel frustrated by the gap between ideas in your head and what you actually manage to put down on paper? Would you prefer it if nobody ever saw what you wrote?

(d) Do you hesitate over reading your tutor's comments in detail? Do you sometimes feel bruised by them? Are you sometimes irritated by them? What are the three most important things you have learnt through your TMA relationship with your tutor?

(e) • Do you find the 'open-endedness' of writing makes you uncomfortable and restless? How does this affect your ability to keep at your writing?

   • Are you gradually finding it easier to 'position yourself' in relation to your imagined 'reader' – to find your 'voice'?

   • Do your essays seem rubbishy when you are about to send them off? Do they seem better when you read them a few months later?

   • Does the essay writing process seem to drag on far too long?

Comment

(a) If it doesn't, you could make a fortune passing on the secret.

(b) Have you managed to get a look at a few essays by other students this year? That's the best way of establishing a sensible point of comparison.

(c) It helps if you can build a bridge between the private and the public, by getting into the habit of exchanging essays with one or two other people, so you get to feel less defensive about what you write and less sensitive about other people's comments. You could still usefully do this before the exam this year. But in any case you can look out for opportunities to do it next year.

(d) We can assure you that the K100 authors experienced just these feelings when colleagues wrote comments all over drafts of units and then aired their views frankly at course team meetings. But we undoubtedly learnt a great deal from the process. Getting advice on writing seems to be one of those 'If it isn't hurting it isn't working' things (to quote John Major). We hope the pain led to progress for you too.

(e) These are aspects of writing which remain problematic, however experienced you become. The point is to work out your own ways of 'managing' yourself, so that you can ride the problems rather than be thrown by them. We hope you feel you are making progress with all four.

Coming to terms with this 'personal' side of writing – the way it makes you feel about yourself and your abilities, the stresses and doubts it gives rise to – is as important as the conceptual and technical skills you have been developing throughout the year.

Writing reports

K100 has focused on developing your essay-writing skills. But how relevant are these skills to the kind of report writing you might have to do in a care situation? How different is a report from an essay? You have read a lot about reports in Block 6, but just to remind you of how varied reports can be, skim quickly back over Activity 6 in Unit 22 (the one with the five reports of Anita Binns's experience at the Adult Training Centre) and the reports you wrote for Activities 2 and 3 in this unit. Now back to how reports differ from essays.

Brevity

Often the most obvious difference is length. People generally have limited time for reading reports. They want the bare essentials for the purposes of the job in hand. A key skill of report writing is to express your points in as few words as possible.

Restricted focus

Reports are usually highly selective in terms of what is included and what left out. This is partly for brevity, but also for clarity (for example what decisions need to be taken) and because it is not appropriate to discuss some things in a professional context, perhaps for reasons of confidentiality or avoiding personal bias. As you saw in Activity 6 in Unit 22, reports of the same event can have very different focuses (in this case the person, the institution, and the process). None of the reports attempted to give a 'rounded' picture. They were addressed to particular concerns and ignored everything else. One of the hardest things when you are new to report writing is learning what you should leave out and what is essential to keep in. For example, if you have to write case notes about someone it is very easy to slip into a biographical style: 'telling the human story'; highlighting personalities, fateful moments and emotional upheavals, while not making clear exactly what problems the case is concerned with; or leaving out, or jumbling up, important details about times and places of treatments, and so on.

Specificity of purpose

The broad purposes of an essay (which tend to remain the same whatever course you study) are to help you explore ideas and to enable your progress to be assessed. The purposes of a report tend to be much more specific to a context. An institution 'requires' the report for a specific reason. Writing it is not an open, creative enterprise. The report has to meet criteria of usefulness and professional correctness. Everything that goes into it needs to be judged against these criteria. Understanding the particular purposes to which your reports will be put is an important part of developing skill in report writing.

Readership and voice

You write essays as one student of the subject presenting an argument to others who may be interested in it. By contrast you write a report as a person in a particular role. You 'speak' in the context of the responsibilities and status of that role. You also address your audience in terms of their role – whether they are clients, junior colleagues, senior colleagues, or members of another professional group. Both your own role and that of your audience determine what is an appropriate 'voice' and tone to adopt. The activity in Unit 22 shows this very clearly. You were probably able to make quite shrewd judgements about who the different versions could have been written by and who they might be written for. Growing into your own role and learning to relate to other people in their roles is an important part of developing an effective report-writing voice.

Activity 9   **Evaluating your own reports**

Allow about 10 minutes   Activities 2 and 3 in this unit asked you to write reports. This activity asks you to evaluate one or both of them in terms of what you have just read about report writing. Read either or both reports again, reminding yourself who the report was intended for, and answer the two following questions.

(a)   Did the report tell your readers all they needed to know using as few words as possible?

(b)   Did the report tell your readers anything they didn't need to know (including anything they didn't have a right to know)?

Comment   You will probably have guessed that if your answer to question (a) was 'yes' and your answer to question (b) was 'no', then your report will have shown the characteristics of brevity, restricted focus and specificity of purpose, and, of course, you will have written a report to meet the needs of its intended readers. If you can work out what the readers of a report need to know, then everything else falls into place.

If you are going to include either of these reports in a portfolio, it would probably be a good idea now to do some editing: putting in anything you have left out which the readers of the report needed to know, and cutting out anything extra.

Skills of report writing

These, then, are some of the main differences between reports and essays. But how different are the skills you need in writing a report? As you have seen, a lot depends on the particular context in which the report is written. Many of the key skills can be fully developed only in a practical situation, where you have a specific role to play and a specific audience to write to. Often reports use a kind of institutional shorthand. They follow a format and style that other reports have used before, so that colleagues know what to look for and where. Instead of spelling things out in full, the writer assumes that colleagues will use their experience to fill in the gaps. To write good reports takes practice in learning the format and style of the particular setting within which you are reporting.

An appropriate format for a report will vary from agency to agency and situation to situation. However, in the context of an OU course, you might write a report, say, on a project you have undertaken. This would be longer and contain more discussion than most work-related reports such as those you wrote for Activities 2 and 3, but it would still be distinctly different from an essay. A major difference is that usually you will be required to organise the report into sections, each with a particular job to do and with its own particular style. Here is a typical structure for a project report.

Introduction. This is an outline of the question(s) the project is investigating and why, making very brief reference back to other studies in the field, to show what your approach is based on. There are no grand claims, no persuasive or emotive flourishes, just sufficient argument to set a framework for what follows (about a paragraph).

Method. This is an outline of why you chose the particular way of gathering information that you did; what you saw as the advantages of this approach as well as what it might leave out; followed by a factual description of the main elements of the investigation, from the early pilot stages to the main data gathering (for example, how many people you interviewed, how you selected them, where you interviewed them, how long for, whether you followed a standard pattern of questions), along with anything that didn't go according to plan and might have influenced the outcome. The style of this section should be as pared down as possible – dry, objective, 'technical', almost like a set of instructions for someone who might want to repeat your study. The length can vary depending on the subtlety of your 'methodology' (your method of enquiry and the assumptions on which it rests), but it could be as little as a page.

Findings. This is often a very challenging section to write because you have to work out how to summarise briefly and simply a lot of very varied information. If you have carried out interviews it might involve quite a lengthy summary of the main types of answer given, including sample quotations. However, if you have used a questionnaire, the section might consist mainly of a table of results. The essence of this section is that it does *not* include any *discussion* of what the findings mean. The aim is to present objective, unvarnished data that stand alone. It should be possible for someone who disagrees with your point of view to read your findings and use them to draw different conclusions.

Discussion. Here you discuss various ways in which the findings might be interpreted. You link them back to the framework for the investigation which you set up in the introduction. And you consider what influences your method might have had on the results. This section is the most like an ordinary essay.

Conclusion. This is a very brief summary of what you set out to investigate and the main conclusions you think can be drawn.

As you can see, a report of this kind involves some very different forms of writing from the discursive essay style. Much of the report is plain, simple, pared-down writing, which aims for objective, accurate description rather than discussion. It takes some practice to develop a polished reporting style, but it isn't a skill on the same scale as learning to write arguments in essays. It doesn't require you to develop a whole new way of thinking and working over a period of several months. It's more a matter of knocking the flourishes off your normal style and fitting into an established framework.

However, beneath the more formal descriptive elements of the report lies (guess what) an argument. It surfaces briefly in the introduction and conclusion and rather more fully in the discussion. It is this argument that holds the report together and gives it strength. So arguing is still a key skill, even though it isn't in evidence at every point in the document. To this extent the skills you develop through your TMAs are highly generalisable. Once you can handle arguments comfortably you can quite quickly become effective in many other kinds of writing.

Study skills: Transferability of arguing skills

The skills which you are developing through essay writing – of arguing a case from evidence – are actually highly relevant to other forms of writing such as report writing. Essays bring the arguing side of writing into the spotlight, making it possible for your tutor to 'coach' you in getting your arguments right. But other forms of writing also present arguments, although often in a more hidden way. As you saw in Unit 22, although reports *look* very different from essays, there is almost always an underlying *purpose* to what is said. In other words a report usually presents an underlying argument of some kind. The terms of the argument are not usually spelt out. In fact, they tend to be assumed as 'obvious', given the circumstances in which the report is written and the audience who will read it. Nevertheless, the writer's basic skill in putting together a convincing case is what gives a report force. The more you develop your techniques of arguing, the better you will be able to select just the few elements you need to deliver punchy reports.

End of block assignment

Now TMA 06 presents you with one last exposure to the challenge of writing, and a final exchange in your 'relationship-through-writing' with your tutor. After all the experience and advice you have received this year and all you have read in *The Good Study Guide*, I hope you feel that you are approaching this essay with a lot more confidence, insight and technique than you brought to TMA 01.

Study skills: Study diary

Just a reminder to bring your study diary up to date, and help yourself to think ahead to Block 7.

3.4 Gearing up to revision

At the end of Block 5 you sketched a rough plan of the last weeks of the course, and marked where you hoped to find your main revision time. You also made a rough estimate of how many revision hours you hope to have overall. Perhaps you have already revisited this plan and begun to refine it. In any case, now is a good time to plan in more detail how you will use your time.

Activity 10

Allow about 45 minutes

A more detailed revision plan

(a)   To get yourself thinking strategically about your approach to revision, read Section 4 of Chapter 7 of *The Good Study Guide*.

(b)   Take a first stab at deciding which blocks of the course you are going to focus on in your revision. (Go back to the comments following Activity 15 in Unit 21 if you need to remind yourself about choosing blocks.)

(c)   Decide whether you will wait until you have finished Block 7 before starting your revision, or whether you will mix revision with studying this new material.

(d)   Decide roughly what percentage of your revision time you think you should give to:

   •   sorting out all your papers, files and materials

   •   going back over your chosen blocks

   •   rereading your essays

   •   practising sketching answers to questions, writing out timed answers, making up questions of your own

   •   group revision with one or more fellow students.

(e)   Work out roughly how many hours you have per block. Mark on your revision plan which day you hope to be doing what. (You may want to draw a fresh plan if the other one is a mess now.)

(f)   Mark down any tutorials, day schools or any other group revision sessions you have arranged.

Comment

(a)   You may find it useful to go back to this section of *The Good Study Guide* several times over the coming weeks, to remind yourself what you are trying to achieve.

(b)   You may change your mind about the blocks as you get back to them. But having an initial plan will help to force the issue about making strategic choices.

(c)   After TMA 06 there is no constraint on how you use your time up to the exam. It may make you feel more confident to begin some revising straight away. It will also help you to become realistic about what you can achieve in the time you have available. But *be sure not to put off Block 7 too late*, or there won't be time to absorb it before you have to write about it. Remember, it is the only block that is 'compulsory' in the exam, and it also includes advice on preparing for the exam.

(d)   Most people would choose to give the bulk of their time to block revision. But this reminds you to leave time for other modes of revision, which can be extremely helpful.

(e)   As the book says, it's very likely that you will have to change your plan as it is overtaken by events. But at least you will be in a position to readjust strategically, rather than simply muddle along.

(f)   Get as much support as you can from working with other people.

If you keep a strategic overview of your revision activities, you should find the coming weeks a very rewarding period of the course. As you look back and revive ideas which were in your mind months ago, and see the connections with what you've done since, you should begin to feel a growing confidence in your new knowledge and a deepening of your understanding. To help it turn out that way, here are two key principles to keep in mind.

   •   *Make revision meaningful and interesting.* Avoid letting it become boring. Seek out ways of making it active, enquiring, creative and varied.

   •   *Play to your strengths.* Build on your interests and experience. Work to patterns that suit you. Don't worry about what you're not – be yourself. You're doing this for you.

Section 4
Linking K100 studies to professional training

Healthcare connections

Information

Healthcare workers need to be aware how complicated and confusing care service provision can seem to potential users and how difficult it is to find out about. They need to be able to think strategically about how to communicate appropriate information about services to potential users, so that it is timely and in a form they can understand. They also need to know how to find out information to carry out their own professional duties. Increasingly the internet is a key resource.

User involvement

Advocacy and self-advocacy promote the development of user-oriented services. However, neither is straightforward. User groups need support and the opportunity to develop advocacy skills.

Records and confidentiality

Healthcare workers are legally required to keep records and manage information, which often has to remain confidential. These records usually serve a variety of functions, for example care plans are also an important part of record keeping for healthcare workers. There can be advantages in involving clients in keeping their own records in partnership with and supported by healthcare professionals. Patients have the right to see their medical records as laid down in the Access to Health Records Act 1990.

Disclosure of information given by NHS patients is governed by doctrines of implicit and explicit consent. Devices to preserve confidentiality include the Data Protection Act (1984), confidentiality policies and professional codes of conduct for healthcare workers. Nevertheless, dilemmas can arise where there is a need to disclose confidential information.

Unit 25 develops skills in interpreting confidentiality policies in difficult situations. These skills could be applied in many healthcare contexts.

Accountability

Issues of accountability have a high profile in healthcare with increased public assertiveness encouraged by initiatives such as the Patients' Charter and Performance Indicators. Problems of accountability in a care setting are discussed in the case studies of Michael and Liam. Healthcare workers manage accountability and risk in many ways including tactics of defensive practice (Reader Chapter 29 and Offprint 32).

Report writing

Healthcare workers need to be able to write succinct, accurate, convincing reports. In Unit 23 you are shown different ways of reporting a particular incident and then in Unit 25 the requirements of effective report writing are discussed in detail.

Social work connections

Service user involvement

Social workers attempt to work in *partnership* with service users. However, enabling service users to become involved can be complex and challenging. One role can be to advocate for users who are trying to become involved in service planning processes, though social workers can be left in a difficult position if service users' views are sought and then not acted upon.

Professional accountability

Social workers are professionally accountable to service users, to their own employers, to the state through legal frameworks and to their professional bodies. Unit 24 looks at structures and processes of accountability and their implications for practice. The *Care Standards Act 2000* established the *General Social Care Council*, to whom social workers are accountable. All social workers now have to be registered with the GSCC.

The role of record keeping

Social workers frequently complain of being overwhelmed with 'red tape' and ever more extensive requirements for record keeping. Unit 23 discusses these concerns, but also stresses the importance of accurate and transparent recording processes. Social workers should not see records as simply a bureaucratic burden but as an essential component of an accountable and ethically sound service.

Confidentiality: rights and responsibilities

A key dimension of an ethically sound and transparent service is that service users have a right to privacy and confidentiality. Information kept by agencies about individuals can have major implications for their lives. Social workers work in agencies with clear guidance on confidentiality. This is supported in law, most recently by the *Human Rights Act 1998*. There are, however, limits to confidentiality. As the NIAS case study demonstrates, there are occasions when social workers are not able to keep information confidential, because to do so would compromise either the safety of that person or other people. How workers think through and negotiate these decisions is an important part of the social work role.

Children and young people: connections

Finding out about services

As with other areas of care, work with children and young people requires knowledge of the services available locally and nationally. The opening of Unit 13 returns to the case of Mandy who, having moved to a new area, is having difficulty connecting with a diversity of agencies and identifying services and support systems relevant to the needs of her son Sean. As Offprint 27 shows, the picture is very complicated and confusing, and Mandy lacks transport, telephone and local knowledge. It is important to understand the barriers between some parents, children, communities and care workers and the information they need. It is also important to develop strategies for disseminating relevant information effectively to those who experience these barriers.

Advocacy and self advocacy

The Unit 22 discussion of advocacy and self-advocacy is of special relevance to work with children and young people, whose position of relative powerlessness and invisibility contributes to their need for committed and effective advocates.

Records

Effective record keeping is particularly important in tracking the health and wellbeing of children, who are otherwise dependent on the judgement and practices of parents, teachers or other responsible adults. A number of prominent cases have shown the damaging and potentially tragic consequences when information about children at risk is not adequately recorded, or passed on between care agencies.

Confidentiality

Confidentiality is an issue too often overlooked in work with children and families. Adults often act as though children have no right to confidentiality, but service providers need to be able to form confidential relationships with the children and young people they work with. For example, back in Unit 14, Sarah Burrows' work on Jamie Knight's life story book required delicate negotiation of the boundaries of privacy as he changed from a boy to an adult. These are complex ethical and practical issues which involve finding a balance between rights and risks. And issues of confidentiality arise not only in working directly with children and young people, but also in working with parents and other responsible adults. Sometimes the right to confidentiality of a parent has to be overridden to protect a child, as you may have decided in the case of Michelle and her baby (Unit 23).

Accountability

As you have seen in cases throughout K100, children and young people are often unable to speak out and be heard when those responsible for their care and support fail to act as they should. This makes accountability a particularly important issue in working with children and young people. Lines of responsibility need to be clearly laid down and procedures established to ensure that bad practice can be brought to light and those responsible held to account.

References

Audit Commission (1994) *Finding a Place: A Review of Mental Health Services for Adults*, TSO, London.

Acknowledgements

Grateful acknowledgement is made to the following source for permission to reproduce material in this unit:

Figure 1: Audit Commission (1994) *Finding a Place: A Review of Mental Health Services for Adults*.